D1250093

Portage, Wisconsin
AND OTHER ESSAYS

BOOKS BY
ZONA GALE

Fiction

MISS LULU BETT

FAINT PERFUME

PREFACE TO A LIFE

BIRTH

YELLOW GENTIANS AND BLUE

WHEN I WAS A LITTLE GIRL

Plays

MISTER PITT

THE NEIGHBORS

MISS LULU BETT

Poems

THE SECRET WAY

Essays

PORTAGE, WISCONSIN AND OTHER ESSAYS

Portage, Wisconsin

AND OTHER ESSAYS

BY

ZONA GALE

NEW YORK

ALFRED · A · KNOPF

1928

MANUFACTURED IN THE UNITED STATES OF AMERICA

To
W · Ll · B

Astronomers and physicists now assure us of man's evolution through geological and zoölogical æons of divine labor, and that our solar system is revolving about the beautiful cluster of Pleiades.

OLD ASTRONOMICAL THEORY

Contents

CHAPTER I
Portage, Wisconsin

ON ONE BANK of a river it should lie — the town that one means when one says "small town." Homes should border the bank, small lawns, sloping to lilacs and willows. The current would be lazy and preoccupied, with leisure for eddies, and daily it would bear old dried trees, dislodged from the up-stream rocks before the first energy of the water had dissolved into meditation. On the opposite shore would be a feathery second growth of maples and hickory-trees, looking as if they must shelter white temples, but really only covering the Bridge farm chicken coops. Beyond would be hills, neatly buttonhole-stitched against a flat horizon, usually gray, sometimes violet, and on occasion ripe pink and yellow, like a cut peach.

On such a scene our back doors and windows look out, as folk occupying box seats. All the older houses have kitchens at the back, with wash-boilers and clothes-reels and wood-piles; but the newer houses have verandas, green shuttered; and "landscape" windows, scrim curtained, as becomes a home which has just discovered that the back door should be the front. The newest houses have a sun parlor, as if they had always had a "view" and had known it. Only we are particular about terms.

For lately a woman from the East, a visitor in the town, paused before a " landscape window " and cried: " Oh what a beautiful vista! " And we told it to one another for days. " *Vista!* "

All we who live on the river sympathize with those who live remote from it. But many of these others once sympathized with us — (" That freezing south wind sweeping across on you. Back street, anyway. Not much of any travel on it.") And if we pointed out that we liked the occasional launches, plying our nonnavigable stream, their alert exhausts, their faded colors, and the ancient row-boats which put off at dusk to stretch unlawful nets near the sand-bar; they said: " Well, you always do make the best of things, anyway." But of late, or since we ride in cars, we all know what a " view " is, and now they say: " You were lucky to have a lot here on the river. How did you come to do that? " And we say that it just happened.

The streets stretch away from us in three directions, and they are bordered by trees. We know that it was Judge Guppey and Mr. Turner who urged upon the town these trees, and that in the common council of those days there was a terrible battle before the planting was done. A woman of seventy, whose home is under those ancient elms, recently rocked on her little porch and observed that her husband was in the common council which voted in the trees. " You must be very proud of that," her visitor said, and she answered with composure and a face unchanging: " Yes. Yes, I am. . . . My husband opposed it at the time. . . ."

Portage, Wisconsin. It seems strange that the majority of the people in the United States have never heard of it. Here it is, with its memories, its traditions, and its settings, and not even the people who pass by on its seventeen through trains daily ever note its name. There is about this circumstance something as piercing as in the look of the visiting-card of a stranger, now dead; or of a nameless photograph on the floor of the attic; or in Milton's line, " The pilot of some small night-foundered skiff."

But we have our revenges. For one midnight I stood at the station and thrilled to see roll on to our tracks a long, sealed train of Pullmans, in whose windows were cards, bearing the two magic words:

Ballet Russe.

For me all Broadway and the metropolitan stage came burning to the West. Those fairy feet so close to our brick platform. . . . And while I looked and marveled, as engines were being changed, one of the station men came by and said: " Some theatrical troupe or other."

In Portage, Wisconsin, there stands an old

church which it was once customary to close
for a month in summer. It was a fair example
of the churches built nearly three-quarters of
a century ago — a kind of blurred Gothic,
with vaulted ceiling, choir alcove, gallery, and
good stained glass. But one September, when
after a month's recess the congregation came
for service, they found their church transformed. Left in his own leisure, the minister
had ceiled over the vaulted roof, masking the
oaken beams by the plaster; had walled up the
choir alcove with its little rose-window; had
torn out the gallery; had replaced the stained
glass windows with white frosted panes. And
to this day, though the church has changed
its religion, these improvements remain.

There was another church which essayed
to close for a vacation. And many live who
remember a young lawyer of the town —
later a judge, and long dead when the town began to be my own — who took some friends
and a crowbar, though neither he nor they
ever entered the church, and drove in the
door, saying: " In all the years I have lived
in this town, the stream of mercy has never
ceased to flow from these doors, and it isn't
going to stop now."

There was a Portage elder with squeaky
shoes who used to pass the plate at service, and
one morning, when the squeak seemed too violent for the solemnity of the ceremony, the

minister spoke aloud and said to him: " Brother
—, you'll find my rubbers out there in the
entry."

But the elder replied, over his shoulder:
" Thank you, I've a pair of rubbers of me
own," and went on passing the plate, and
squeaking.

Of late a Portage church wished to give a
pageant, celebrating the seventy-fifth anniver-
sary of its founding. But when the church
history was reviewed, these and other bits were
recalled which could not properly be included
in the pageant and in fact have no place in
church history at all, but only in the profane.
As of the wife of the judge who wore little
pink shells in her ears to augment her hearing,
and when she bent her head to the back of the
seat before her, in prayer, the shells always fell
out, and her grandchildren spent the prayer
hour scrambling about the floor, recovering
them.

Of the mice in the choir, where the women
sat swinging handkerchiefs, as they listened
and as they prayed.

Of the melodeon which was accustomed, in
crises, to shed a peg in its bellows; and when
this occurred, it was the duty of the contralto
to turn, stoop, and replace the peg, but to
keep on singing and never miss a note. Of the
tenor, the choir leader, who during the sermon
retired to the choir-loft stairs and slept; and

a part of the Sunday duties of the same contralto was to go down and wake him up in
time for the last hymn.

Of the little girl in the infant class. This
class, one morning, the school superintendent
passed just as they were all singing:

> " I want to be an angel
> And with the angels stand,
> A crown upon my forehead,
> A harp within my hand."

" Beautiful," said the superintendent,
deeply moved. " And does every little girl and
boy here want to be an angel? "

On which this little girl said to all: " I
don't. I'd rather be a monkey and swing by my
tail."

In the church was an uncle of the little
girl's, who was reminded of a happening of his
youth in Vermont, where a Sunday-school superintendent was impressing on the school the
names of those with Jesus on the mount of
transfiguration. In the town lived a family
named Danhouse, whose four sons were
named Peter, James, John, and Henry. So the
superintendent shamelessly used association as
an aid to memory, and said: " You can remember who was there by the Danhouse boys
— Peter, James, and John." When in the review at the end of the hour, he asked who
else was on the mount of transfiguration, up

went a hand and a confident voice called out:
" All the Danhouses but Hank."

I wish that this story had belonged to Portage itself instead of merely to the youth of a
Portage uncle.

My own chief conscious contribution to
such annals occurred at a Christmas entertainment, when I was to recite " Ring Out, Wild
Bells." On the night of nights I began about
the third stanza to waver. But I liked reciting
and had no mind to stop, so, depending on the
recurrence of the refrain to buoy up the lines,
I recall inserting words and phrases, and repeti-
tions — regardless of what the poet wanted
rung out and what rung in:

> " . . . love, hope joy, joy.
>   Ring out, wild bells,
>   Courage and hope and love and joy,
>   The flying cloud, the frosty night,
>   Ring out, ring out, ring out, wild bells,
>   Ring out, wild bells, and let them die."

I had the stage, and nobody knew the difference who was rude enough to say so. The conscience of the prompter afterwards troubled
her, and she apologized to my mother for losing the place. It was the first free verse ever
introduced into Portage, Wisconsin.

THE WHOLE locality has a treasure of funeral
lore.

In this the small towns have antedated the

skepticism of the larger, which no longer wail and hire mourners, but which perhaps still have scant lore of funeral jokes. In the metropolitan theaters, for example, the elision of such humor is in obedience to some tenet of art dictated by audiences: for in the ebb and flow of scenes, in the building to crests and peaks, it is well known that even a slant mention of death will send the listeners down a great steep, and kill the scene. This is not true in clubs and smokers. It may be that the small town corresponds to a club. For here, early in the history of the town, funerals must have been a rich source of anecdote, since so many survive. One, of a layman who was to speak at the burial of a townsman, and who leaned on the pulpit and thus began: " I was well acquainted with the deceased, with that gentleman down there," and pointed with his thumb to the casket below. And there is a memory of the choir at a funeral singing lustily:

> " One sweet flower has drooped and faded,
> One dear infant's voice has fled.
> One fair brow the grave has shaded,
> One dear school-mate now is dead.
>
> " But we feel no thought of sadness,
> For our friend is happy now,
> Knowing naught but heart-felt gladness
> Where the holy angels bow "

— and of the soprano at this point going off into sobs in which the whole choir joined.

It was in a town to the south of us that a minister of that period, preaching a funeral sermon for a farmer, cried out, in a strong singsong, compounded of equal parts of drawling and of lightning rapidity: " He's gone. He's gone. Nevermore-shall-you-hear-his-voice-at-the-foot-of-the-stairs c r y i n g : ' Hul*day*! Hul*day! Get* up. *Get* breakfast. He's gone.''

It was in a town to the west of us that in those days a woman telephoned to a livery stable to ask for the " little blacks " and was told that she would have to take the little bays because the little blacks had gone to the funeral. But when, in half an hour, the carriage arrived, it was drawn by the little blacks; and when she questioned the driver, she heard: " Well, the blacks was standing right acrost the street outside the church, hitched to the hearse. So I just went and took out the blacks and put in the bays. I says to myself: ' The corp won't care.' ''

OUR SOCIAL consciousness, like that of most of our national neighbors, wakes slowly. When the town first talked of sewerage, there were those who said to us: " But *you* have the river — what do you care whether they get sewerage or not? ''

When tuberculin-tested milk became the leading precaution, and we inquired of our milkman whether his cows had ever been tested, he replied proudly: " No, ma'am. Nothing of that kind has ever been necessary."

When the schools introduced domestic science, there was a mother of a first family who said: " It is unnecessary. My daughters can learn all the domestic science they need right at home." Quite like the Italian mother in Jones Street, who forbade her child to attend the dental clinic at Greenwich House, saying: " Rosie shouldn't get all her teeth pulled out." Or like the metropolitan kindergarten which at first struggled against the belief that its sponsors were trying to get their children off their hands.

(It is fascinating to live in the town where you first went to kindergarten — as in the basement of the Trinitatis Church, a few blocks from the river. To pass that building with its old square brown " steeple " is to recover the very air of that hour when, leaving the others, one went off by oneself, away round the church, and, by the far front door-stone, came on a blazing yellow buttercup, growing alone in the long, bright grass. There is the door-stone, in proof, today. One passes it.)

If our social consciousness as a whole awakens slowly, it has its brief flares of brilliance too. It flared and died, some years ago, in a rest room for farmers' wives, in the city hall, furnished by a common effort. But when one day a bake sale was held there, the common council adjourned in a body to the rest room, inspected it, saw a second-hand metal box bestowed by a hardware store and a gas jet used to heat the babies' milk, returned, and passed an order rescinding its permission to use the room, since " the women were baking in there." Now rest rooms are required by Wisconsin law, in towns exceeding five thousand. We are one of the few towns of our size to have garbage collection, a system which grew over the initial protest of a city father who cried: " Ain't that always done private? "

But the hospital, the library, the new high school, the one street of asphalt, the white way, are as much a part of the slow awakening of the common consciousness of the people as is the completion of the Chicago boulevards with its made land in Lake Michigan; or our common sharing of the upper air, plowed by the wings of planes.

We too are losing the slow heresy of " I am " and reaching to the racial certainty that " we are." And it is a moving thing to watch the esoteric teaching of group consciousness arrive among us by " town improvement associations " as well as by the religious teaching of brotherhood. By the wife of the mayor who, with her neighbors, went down with a wooden

rake and helped to clear up the market square
for planting. And by that church organist
who cried: " Yes! Let's buy a galvanized tank
for garbage collection, and if we can't af-
ford a driver, we can drive it ourselves! " By
the woman's club which took to studying its
town and determined how often the blankets
at the " calaboose " were washed. And by the
birth of the little park at a bridge end, out
of Frances Hodgson Burnett's remitted roy-
alty on a local performance of *The Dawn of
a To-morrow,* a generosity matched by the
townspeople who, hearing of this, gave theater, light, coal, printing, everything; and the
resultant shrubbery and paths and sward slope
to the water and to the west, unto this day.

VESTIGES OF Puritanism, one might believe
them to be, certain renunciations, certain re-
fusals to make common use of perishable pos-
sessions. They have another genesis. The Pais-
ley, the Spanish shawl, the frail scarf, the jewel,
the china, all are laid away on the closet shelf
or in the cupboard and never brought forth
save to show briefly, and to wrap up again.
Questioned as to why these things should not
be used, the answer is: " When I want something nice, I'll have it."

The life-saving foundation of the pioneer
thrift thus survives its necessities.

There was here a woman of means who, on

being told that her skirt was crooked, replied:
" I know it. It's shabby in front, so I moved
it around."

Not here, but in a more beautiful Wisconsin
town, there was received this letter by neighbor, from neighbor:

" Dear Cora,
" My door bell got out of order so I had to get a hard-
ware man to fix it.
" Please turn it about half way over, *and I can hear*
that *all over my house.*
" You always ring it too hard. *I must be careful of it*
now.

" With love
" — — "

It is nowhere more evident than in a little town that our chief art-expression is
through humor. If a song were a fraction so
common as humor, we should go singing all
day long.

As it is, we laugh — from tea-party to grocery store, from council meeting to railway
station, everyone has a jest to give and to take.
Perhaps this has a deeper significance than we
allow. Perhaps it touches on Stevenson's phrase
of something " real, like laughter "; laughter
as a social pastime in rhythm with the emerging social faculties — mounting in importance *and thereafter falling.* First the jest of
the yokel, then the shrewd humor of the
countryman; first the empty laughter of

small-town good nature, then delicious native humor without inhibitions; first the crass restaurant or tea cackle of the sophisticated; then the subtle intellectualized wit of the urbane. Always the first in every pair of these opposites demands laughter, clamors for it, is injured if laughter is not forthcoming. And so it is in a last stage of all—in the present slant downward — when completely socialized laughter demands too its incessant laughter antiphonal. It may be, however, that we are mounting again, as a race, since there are those who find it boring to be expected to laugh *all* the time — though that may be only our dour Scotch blood showing through. Although such laughter may eventually go the way of hand-clapping and disappear, for the present we in Portage find ourselves still delighting in delicious native humor, without inhibitions.

WE HAVE our charming illogicalities. Why must the living-room table be kept clear of objects? So that there will be room if one wants to lay something down.

We hear: "Don't use a curling-iron on your hair — I used to use one on mine. It never hurt it any, though."

And: "Don't get the candy at Blank's. I had some the other day that I couldn't eat. It didn't come from there, though."

And: "Which side of the double house do they live in?" "There's only one side, and they live in the other."

And a delicious unconscious wit, as: "I'm not going to bake pancakes with the family coming to breakfast in giblets."

There was here a woman of English descent, tall and of dignity and beauty, whose humor was a mine to her friends. She said: "I'm not going to have that picture here in the living-room any longer. I'm going to put it in my bedroom. I don't know whether it's a bedroom picture. . . ."

"What is a bedroom picture?" she was asked.

And she answered: "Oh, a nymph, with mushrooms."

On being urged to go on an expedition, she cried: "I never saw anything like you. You're never satisfied unless you're going from Shem to Gomorrah."

And there was a day when she cried gaily: "I'm *damn*termined to do this."

It was a householder whose wife was ingenious in disguising revised dishes who, seated at dinner before a chicken in its third incarnation, observed dryly: "This chicken wears well, doesn't it?"

Our arguments on pronunciation are continual. One was concerning "rind," which was declared by one proponent to have a short *i*; and after a fiery discussion this short-vowel advocate compromised. " Well," said he, " it's rĭnd when it's on cheese and it's rind when it's off."

There is no dinner-table wit elsewhere that can delight me as do these comments here. As, " Some people never can go to a picnic without turning it into an Indian massacre. . . ." " Her home is furnished different, with things all carved and hard to dust. . . ." " I don't care much for style, but I do like to be dressed so that I don't have to stand with my back to the wall, on account of some reason or other. . . ." " Throw back your shoulders; you have to, to bring out the real set of the coat." " I never heard him do a thing decisive except to sneeze. . . ." " A man that always says ' coffin ' and ' devil' right out, instead of 'casket' and 'the Evil One.' . . ." "She's too busy tending to her children to give them much attention. . . ." " It seems like a party when you get your bread thin. . . ." " He thinks if he keeps at a distance and kisses nobody, his germs will all flock round him and not cross the room. . . ." " I don't know what the bird was. It made a noise between a mourning dove and a lawn-mower. . . ." " You saw her great interest in my library. Do you think she cares for books? *No*. She was hunting for dust on the top leaves. I know her. . . ." " She is a graduate in art. She took the whole course in china painting. . . ." " I can remember the time when not even the birth of a child was mentioned in the newspaper — nothing that had anything of a *tang* to it."

And exasperated by the persistent resignation and cheer of a neighbor, a woman burst out: "You'd think it was pretty in hell. You'd say: ' Devil, devil, isn't that a beautiful flame? "

(BUT WE would not have it thought that New York is behind us in comment. As those quoted words are bona-fide Portage, so these are bona-fide Manhattan: It was a beautiful woman of middle age at tea at Sherry's who said: " I suppose you read all the new books as they come out? " It was a cosmopolitan of three continents who said to a lady whose hearing was affected: " Good-bye, Mrs. —. I hope that I have been able to speak loud enough to make you hear." And when that lady, in explanation, had once said: " I hope you don't think that I am as stupid as I seem, but I don't hear very well," it was another New Yorker who replied brightly: " Oh, that's it! ")

THE WORD "mother " has a correspondence in nature, beyond the individual and beyond the possessive. This word appears to signify some spiritual condition which is to the macrocosm what mother is to the human atom.

Maternity is less a relationship than an extra-physical force, to which shocking violence has been done by children — through sentimentality, and by mothers — through monarchy.

In this wise it is that, to one born and bred there, a town may be less a place than a force, less a force than a fragrance. Particularly is this true of a small town, as one can be more moved by a puppy of one's own than by anybody else's lion. And the two words " Portage, Wisconsin " have become for me mesmerized, as have certain words of power in which orientals and others find potency, words which through immemorial repetition by the devout have become charged. So these two words, having been written down by me thousands of times, are for me charged words, and do something which the words " Vienna," " Paris," " Pasadena," and " Calcutta " cannot accomplish; for such words I have not entered upon, nor have they created in me their current.

There is more to this condition than we suppose. May it not be that one born and bred in a town, and rooted there by ties, by houses in which one has lived, by childhood, by first school, and by a grave — may it not be that such an one does actually see that town heightened, drawn through into deeper perception, adjusted to contacts not only of the eye and the memory, but of other and far more sensitive cells and powers?

I have looked out on the Wisconsin River flowing at the foot of our lawn, at the Caledonia hills carving the sky-line, and have wondered if these are as beautiful as I believe them to be, and how a stranger would regard these. And now I wonder whether there is here involved a consideration not of emotion, not of the group soul — but rather of a new physics intimating that love-association does actually unveil properties and perhaps surfaces unknown to the sense of the casual passer-by.

CHAPTER II
Katytown in the Eighties

IN THE LATE EIGHTIES, Chautauqua Literary and Scientific Circles — C.L.S.C.'s, as they were intimately known, — were in their full flower in the United States. It was thrilling to see middle-aged men and women responding to the treasuries of academic commonplace, minds coming, adult yet virgin, to Ulysses and Goethe and Juno and Runnymede.

I remember sitting silent on a little carpet-covered stool and listening to a woman named Lucy Lovejoy relate to my mother a part of the epilogue to the American Revolution.

" And, look here, in the first place they never wanted to *u*-nite at all. No, sir! Some of 'em said it was impossible the colonies should ever be got to *u*-nite. Yes, sir! And when they first talked it, to a meeting in Albany, only seven colonies sent delegates and nobody much but Benjamin Franklin was what you might say hot for it. Did you ever hear of such a thing? But the Governor of Massachusetts, he wanted it in order to fight France. And say! The folks in Massachusetts was jealous of the folks in Virginia, and Georgia and South Carolina most fit over usin' the Savannah River. And, Mrs. Gale, when them first British troops come over, they tented 'em on the Boston

Common, and our book says Samuel Adams
got up in the Old South Church and he says:
' This meeting can do nothing more to save the
country ' . . . wait till I tell you: *that* was
when we dumped the tea — wasn't it grand?
Fifty men, got up like Mohawk Indians, done
it. And Paul Revere, he rode off to Philadelphia
to tell 'em the jig was up. . . ."

She poured it out with spirit, she was bright-
eyed, she had on either cheek a little high red
spot. All her facts had been unknown earth
until the Chautauqua American History had
opened to her. And now gossip, domestic grievances, prices, had all been dropped from her
conversation. She was enthralled, as by the fiction that she had never learned to love. Her
dining-room wall was covered with her diplomas, she counted for you their seals. In a hundred homes of the nation it was the same.
There was, in the eighties, a homely renais-
sance, not of learning, but of study. It was as
if the grammar-school had waked and cried its
commonplace aloud, beyond its walls. And this
commonplace was now no longer in its dis-
guise of task, of penance; but was at last radiant, clothed with its essential wonder.

Women of the Middle-West university and
college towns were ardent in the movement,
as became those whose look had long been toward the thresholds which they had never
crossed. And the little near-by towns had their

circles, meeting on winter evenings, when coal
stoves glowed and on hot summer afternoons,
when muslin curtains stirred. All the stimuli
were there — the love of learning, latent in
the pioneer and waiting the mellower time
when it might flower; the social urge to work
together; the zest of competition in the race
for seals and courses completed; and, sharpest
of all, the dumb desire to " keep up " with the
young folk, already coming home from school
with challenging inquiries. Secret in the heart
of this whole phenomenon lay all the time this
imperative object, and glorified it, yet not
more, after all, than it was glorified by the
mere subjective desire to know.

To Katytown the C.L.S.C. came not as a
process, but as a power. Thirty women were
caught up by it and straightway looked
through windows where had been but walls.
These were the days when marketing and
household work made the morning, sewing
and calling the afternoon; and evening ended
early. " Company for supper " and driving
were the chief entertainment. The machinery
of a livelihood was all-absorbing. Children and
love and the out-of-doors were the magic. But
the C.L.S.C. gave upon the outer world.

The Katytown circle was made up of both
men and women; rather, of women and those
husbands who could be allured to attend. There
were young matrons whose husbands were

occasionally to be induced to the meetings, but growling neolithic growls. There were older — and stiller — women of simplicity, not the sad, feigned simplicity of a later time, but of a simplicity native and unconscious; women of some tradition they were, with inherited nests of tables, women whose husbands slept through the entire evening. Ministers and the school principal always attended and were deferred to in any perplexities — foreign phrases, Biblical and geographical names, subjunctives; and if in the lesson there occurred anything of indelicacy (" anything with a tang to it," they said), by common consent it was maneuvered to the minister, who read it in the temper of the Hebraic embarrassments, so that one thought nothing of it, or not more than when he rhymed " wound " with " sound," as he always did.

A half-dozen women there were whose husbands flatly declined to attend. (" He is pretty tired when night comes." " He says: ' Of course I'll go if you say so, but . . . ' and I haven't the heart to make him." " He likes to have me go, but he's a great hand to stay away from everything." And occasionally, with a confidential forward leaning: " He does hate to change his clothes.")

Consider an evening on which the C.L.S.C. met with Mis' Artemus Mason. Mis' Mason had double parlors, cut by an arched doorway, heavily moulded and painted gray-white. Precisely in this archway was stationed the coalstove — a base-burner, showing ruddy from the snowy street. It was October, and it had not been necessary to light the coal (to " fire up," as they said), but the stove had been specially set up, lest this evening prove chilly. The hostess explained this to everyone on arrival. (" Perhaps you do feel chilly. Wouldn't you like a little shoulder shawl? ") These rooms were high ceiled, hung with " golden floral " wall-paper and with stiff lace curtains spread fan-shape on the Wilton carpet. There was a square piano, there was a towering old secretary, whose shelves were filled with Compendiums of Useful Knowledge, Great Truths by Great Authors, Hill's *Manual,* Tupper, Morse, Hall, Matthews. There was a blackwalnut center-table with finials on the carved cross-pieces and a round felt mat, pinked at the edge and beaded in Greek design. There were camp-chairs covered with Brussels. The ornaments were in keeping: on the white marble mantel stood a writing-urn, and from the high bronze and black hanging lamp hung an ostrich egg, painted with cat-tails. This lamp someone was intermittently lifting and lowering, and the weights scraped. It was before the days of Rochester burners, but there were double wicks on reading-lamps, and one wick was forever flaring up on the table lamp of pink frosted glass, and every time that it flared, like cats' ears, the hostess murmured something about it, as if she were at fault. The rooms both smelled a little of the kerosene.

The hostess called the meeting to order. (" Friends, if you please . . ." did that). She was a little woman of fifty, with gray hair drawn high at the temples, and with thin central frizzings. She was wearing a wine-colored stuff gown, with a wine velvet " vest " front, and she had on two cameo rings, both too loose, and a watch and chain. Her head had a pretty sidewise droop, and she had an engaging smile and a way of looking up — graces without homage, save in her brief flowering at courtship time. She was flushed in her double capacity, for the circle was accustomed to meet with the member who was to prepare the paper. Mr. Mason, a slow-moving attentive man, had been admitting the guests, and though the bell — set on the outside of the door below the wrought-iron panels — though the bell went off like a pistol every time that it was pulled Mis' Mason could call: " Edward! The bell! " — and he already moving toward it. This man had a smooth-shaven upper lip, a beard, and a bald head — as if no one had been there to distribute things aright. From the moment when order was bespoken, little giggles came from the hall. There on the draughty stairway, and peering through the balustrade spindles, was a minister's little boy and another minister's little girl, amused out of all proportion to the simple happenings.

Mis' Mason called on Miss Lelah Parkinson to open the program with a piano selection. Mis' Mason explained that the piano was a little out of tune and Miss Parkinson explained that she was a little out of practice. She had on long ear rings terminating in gold fringes and bobbing to the motions of her head which swayed lightly to her rhythms. She played the *Mountain Bell Schottische*.

The previous year the circle had completed *The Preparatory Greek Course in English,* and was now centering upon *The Preparatory Latin Course in English*. Each household in the circle had a copy of the text-book, and the text, which everyone was to have read once or twice in the course of the week, was followed by all, so far as the hanging lamp and the frosted lamp with the double wick would permit, while Mis' Mason read aloud:

" ' The present volume is, in order of preparation and publication, the second one in a series of four books devoted, all of them, to the same general purpose. That purpose is to conduct readers, by means of the English tongue alone, through substantially the same course of discipline in Greek and Latin literature — not, observe, Greek and Latin, the languages, but Greek and Latin literature — as is accomplished by students who are graduated from our American colleges. . . . If we ourselves, therefore, do not, in preparing this volume, fall short of our mark, whoever reads this volume with suitable attention will, having so read it, be as well informed in the literature of the Romans as are students who have triumphantly passed their entrance examinations for college and have thus become duly numbered in the ranks of proud and happy freshmen. The present volume bears the title *Preparatory Latin Course in English.* . . .[1]

" ' The watchful reader will have noticed that we make a distinction. We say Greek and Latin literature — not Greek and Latin, the languages themselves. We do not hope and aim to make linguists of our readers. Greek and Latin scholars they will not become, however heedfully they may read these books of ours. . . . No reader need now misunderstand us. Our aim is a practical one. It is not on our part foolishly aspiring. It should breed no foolish conceit on the part of any reader. No truly intelligent reader of our books will ever be found boasting that he has come to knowledge of Greek and Latin by a royal road. . . . We say there is no royal road to Greek and Latin scholarship. Whatever flattering opinion you, dear reader that have never studied Greek and Latin, may kindly entertain of the road we build for you — call it royal, if you please, and many thanks for your goodwill — still, let there be no mistake as to whither the road built by us leads. It does not lead to knowledge of Greek and Latin, but only to some real knowledge of Greek and Latin letters. You will indeed be able to talk with college-bred men and women on a tolerable footing of equality, about Greek books and Latin. But when it comes to a comparison of your knowledge with theirs, in the matter of Greek and Latin, you will discreetly and modestly be silent. You may inwardly suspect — and one chance at least in ten your suspicion will be correct — that your graduate

---

[1] *Preparatory Latin Course in English.* Chautauqua Press, 1886.

friends too might better be silent themselves than loquacious, on these same delicate topics of accurate scholarship. But that fact let college-bred people themselves be the ones to avow. Enough for you, not disputing the avowal when made, quietly to enjoy the substantial satisfaction of conscious peerage with the liberally educated in familiarity with ancient classic literature.

" ' We shall be gratefully glad if we may feel ourselves to be, in the endeavor to make our books faultless, of one guild and fellowship with all our readers. . . . It is a loaded table of contents to spread in a single volume before our readers. But we trust their appetite, as we shall have to ask them to trust our cookery. It will, we confess it beforehand, be the fault of the cook if the feast is disappointing. . . . Now forward.' "

Mis' Artemus Mason read well, and she knew it. She had the reputation of being " up " on pronunciation, and she made a point of that position. Often callers at her house have seen her pause with uplifted finger, and, " Now, do you know, I can *not* be sure that I am correct on that," she would say, and she would go to her Webster's Unabridged in the parlor, and emerge with the news. Also, " I'll look it up in the *Encyclopædia Britannica,*" you often heard her promising. So she packed into the race her anxious molecule of respect for the content of every word of her language. And tonight her only fault was her virtuous faultlessness. Unless one ungraciously includes a tendency to the apostrophe, as " flatt'ring," " bett'ring." And if she mis-spoke, she met the moment prettily with a nod of the head a little sidewise and " Well! " For an hour she read, uninterrupted save by occasional sibilants from the staircase where well outside the spell of Latin literature the two sat delighting at nothings and now and then fell down a step or more. Also Mr. Artemus Mason remembered that he had not covered the canary with a newspaper and, lest the bird wake and cause a diversion by singing, he himself caused a diversion by picking his way to the cage among the readers. The gentlemen watched him. Other gentlemen wakened. On the whole, the interval was not unwelcome, save to Mis' Mason, who, however, said nothing, though perhaps not permanently.

Following the reading there was opportunity for discussion. Mis' Mason closed the book and waited brightly. After a silence, " Let us hear from a number tonight," she said. No one said anything. There had been, at the cessation of the reading, a moment of pleasantly relaxed tension, when Mr. Enos Abbott, one of the older members, had frankly yawned aloud, and had been cut off in some zenith by his wife, clutching informally at his leg, and had gone, diminuendo, into a smothered but articulate " Wha's the matter? ". Now, however, the tension caught them all again, and they waited for Mr. Becker. Mr. Becker always spoke first. In Chautauqua discussions, in prayer-meeting, on committees, it was the same. He was inherently and fundamentally a chairman. Mr. Becker looked like Jonathan Swift.

"Very edifying," said he, "most edifying. I have been singularly interested in following the present reading. I — of course none of us are as familiar with Roman letters as we might become. I — the present plan seems to offer a very, very neat entrance into those — ah — mysterious, I may say, emblems. I recall as a boy being drawn to read considerable about Cicero. Remarkable man, Cicero — a very remarkable man. I — my reading has somewhat gone from me, I confess, and a chance to brush up will be very, very acceptable. I — none of us, I should think, need be ashamed of a desire to penetrate to these — ah — portals, at this time."

He sat down, folded his coat about him, sighed, caught his lips tightly together, lifted his brow, and gazed thoughtfully down, over his folded arms. Somehow, the doors to art and letters had closed just before he reached them, but he had never understood that he was outside.

"That's true," said Mis' Mason, nodding. "Now someone else? Isn't there?"

Elbert Morehouse was an old lawyer who usually spoke at some length, and there was, as he rose, a certain apprehension. He tasted his lips slowly, and consulted the picture-moulding.

" My study of the Greek and Latin tongues," said he, " in my college days has proved a great source of satisfaction to me. I remember I didn't like them at the time — had to be forced into them by my desire to complete my prescribed course, I recall. But I am thankful for the little I had, since it gave me my only glimpse into that plane of classic letters. It is a great world on which we are about to enter, my friends, and we ought to enter in reverence, in reverence. There is a shadow of a mighty destiny upon that race of the Romans — a destiny never realized in its plenitude, but all too plainly mapped out by the — ah — prowess of the people. What names! How the mind staggers back at their very syllables! Cæsar, a man who . . ."

He went through a catalogue of names, rolling them with a certain authentic tenderness. A passionate reverence, blind and unrooted, was in him and made itself evident. He would have liked to know how to love those names, and he did love something. But it was not that which he was expressing. On the stairs those two put their heads down and giggled at the sound of his periods.

He was succeeded by another pause, which Mis' Mason, rocking slightly in her patent rocker, bridged with a bright: " Anyone else? Let the discussion be free."

One of the older women now spoke — a gentle, delicate woman, with blue veins in her temples, and a smile which, given in nervousness, was yet rare and lovely.

" It seems to me," she said, " that one of the things I shall be most thankful for is to know all those references when I come to them. I was reading ahead in the book this afternoon, after I got my lesson. I never knew about Cornelia and her two Gracchi — is that the way you pronounce it? " (It was not.) " And I've often seen the name ' Ovid ' and so on. I think it makes you feel so inferior not to know what those words mean. My father knew quite a good deal of Latin," she added, and sat down.

" Oh, that makes me think of something I found in the book today, farther on," said Mis' Mason. " I just can *not* keep from reading ahead after I get my lesson." She made a search and after several false starts, she read:

" ' Any Latin reader is pretty sure to contain its share of fables and anecdotes. . . . The tyro ' (I think that's ' tyro ') ' is constantly allured along the paths of Latin lore by some appetizing bit, of tale, of witty wisdom, held out before him. . . . The sweet juice of the meaning is usually well diluted in the youthful student's mouth with the secretions of his own mental idiosyncrasy, excited to flow by the long suspense of ruminant mastication necessary before the mingled product is ready to be swallowed and entered into his hungry, individual circulation. On the whole, the Latin Reader (ask any college graduate) is saturate with pleasureable association.' " [2]

" Isn't that beautiful? " murmured a little woman near to Mis' Mason.

A younger woman looked up with the air of a ripe peach, fresh from sleep.

" It seems to me," she said, " that this Mr. What's-name who wrote this book has some pretty nice thoughts himself."

In the murmur of assent a woman named Mis' Helmus Copper, and quite generally known as Mis' Hellie Copper, stirred abruptly and spoke for the first time: " Well, it seems to me," said she, " that he does an awful lot of talking that I could worm along without."

This they took tolerantly, with a smile, as being " just like Mis' Hellie Copper."

They were to hear yet once more from the book when the high-school principal had spoken. He was a man of fifty, with that manner of positiveness consequent to long speaking down to others, a manner rather dictatorial than academic. He would not have said: " I present the following thesis." He would have said: " I want you to bear in mind. . . ." He now said that it was to him a regret that this outline of study might not have yielded some insight into the Roman tongue — a never-failing source of inspiration through

[2] Ibid.

life. He referred to his satisfaction in tracing
the English words to their Latin derivatives.
He gave some instances. The two on the stairs
were in ecstasies of mirth at this sight, in
private life, of a man who did not belong
there, but on a rostrum.

" Isn't that wonderful? " said the ripe and
wakened peach. " I never thought of that in
my life before. Think of ' cordial ' being from
the Latin word meaning heart. Oh, isn't that
wonderful? "

Her work — she was etching a splasher
of frogs and cat-tails, done in red cotton —
dropped to her knee; her face was lighted,
radiant.

" Oh," cried Mis' Mason, " that's the very
thing the book advises. I found it today.
Wait," she entreated everyone, " wait a minute." She searched, ran it down, read:

" ' To all readers, whatever their private motive,
who would gladly furnish themselves with a modest
but serviceable smatter of Latin, we take great pleasure
in saying your wish can be gratified. . . . You have
no new alphabet to learn. A Latin page does not like
the Greek bristle to you with Procul, Procul ' (if that's
what it is) ' Off, Off, multitudinously horrid in the very
aspect of the letters. . . . Very well, go at it, nothing
doubting. Read it unafraid. . . . Skip paragraphs, pages
even. . . . Get yourself thus easily led up to the declen-
sions, so-called, of the Latin nouns. Fall afoul of these.
. . . You can make singsong of the task and chant it as
an accompaniment to any necessary other employment

you may happen to have in hand. . . . Once more
unto the breach, dear friends, and storm the four conju-
gations of the Latin verbs. There, that is all. Only, of
course, you can, you know, if you find you really like
Latin grammar, look, as much as pleases you, at the rules
of syntax. But you will now have learned enough Latin
to serve useful ends.' " [3]

"I read that too," said one of the older
women. "And I thought I'd do it. I could
learn those what's-names while I'm ironing."

"And then think!" cried another. "You
could take an English page and pick out the
different words that came out of Latin."

"What good'd that do you?" demanded
Mis' Hellie Copper.

"Why, so to know!" cried two or three
together.

Mis' Arthur Mason placed the cap-stone.

"Well," she said, "and then it makes you
feel as if Katytown isn't all there is to it."

And there, it may be, you have the secret of
the success of the Chautauqua movement, in
Katytown and everywhere else. As exoteric
Christianity gave to slaves a dream of eternal
rest; as the India service or any war gives to
task-ridden boys the hope of change and adventure; as music opens a door upon beauty,
and the life of the spirit quickens to new levels
of perception and faculty, so areas of drudgery and rounds of hackneyed thought were
abruptly lit by the splendid suspicion that this

[3] Ibid.

wasn't all of it. Years too late to respond to
Aladdin and Alice, they cried hail and farewell
to Ganymede and glyptodons and Gilbert à
Kempis and his Saracen lady.

Here was one of the high romances of education in the United States, romance to be
classed with the initial passion which laid the
foundations of public school and university
in the wilderness; and with the day- and
night-schools for eager aliens and mountain
folk; and with the woman's-club movement
of the nineties, before it concerned itself with
civic and social betterment. For in the
C.L.S.C., as in the woman's-club movement
growing out of it, inhered the social factor of
contagion. It was one of those inexplicable
psychological phenomena of a large part of
the population becoming subject to nothing
new, nothing which it might not itself have
claimed. The mere spell of suggestion set the
thousands to buying books, holding meetings,
taking examinations, framing diplomas, ex-
hibiting seals, graduating. . . .

Very far away they all were to those two
whispering on the stairs at Mis' Artemus
Mason's. All those folk seemed concerned with
gray territories and remote. Let a hush fall
and it was, to those two, comic, excruciating.
They would bury their faces and think that
they tried not to laugh. For what did they two
know of life? And what do any know of life

who fail to understand those meetings on winter evenings in the eighties?

The romance of the time has not yet been equalled among the women of the middle class in the United States. They had answered to a faint tocsin which, in the present pealing clamor of their bells, the twenty million women of the country may as well remember.

CHAPTER III
"Father" [1]

His FIRST MOMENT of high consciousness came in the fifties in a watermelon patch. Stooping above ripe melons one September night, a half-dozen boys about him, he was struck by the difference, and lifted his face. The sky was flowing with light. In the zenith floated a crown from which poured tides of color. He had not heard of the aurora. The experience was not unlike vision.

When he is asked: " Did you stop eating melons? " he replies: " Oh, no. But I ate them — and looked up."

From that moment his faculties reported for him on new areas. The sky became as important as the creek. He knew a night, still tonic to his thought, when he saw, as he crossed the orchard with his uncle, a star hung between the horns of the new moon.

He says: " I know that this is impossible. But I saw it. We both saw it. We were on our way to bed down the horses, and we stood still and looked at that star between the horns of the moon."

[1] Charles F. Gale, born Galetown, Green Creek Township, Sandusky County, Ohio, August 25, 1842; son of Franklin Gale, born Lynn, Massachusetts, and of Sallie (Ray) Gale of Pittsford, New York. Eighth generation in descent from Richard Gael, who in 1640 settled in Watertown, Massachusetts, and in 1660 on the Oldham Farm, where the town of Waltham now stands.

His father had died when the boy was six.
Now that he was seven, his mother "went,"
as they said. For him old echoes of the family
sounded. As of that old New England grandfather who had, against tremendous national-
istic odds, gone about reiterating: " I am Irish
from the crown of my head to the sole of
my feet." North of Ireland, Scotch-Irish descent, others had related. Then England. Then
Massachusetts in 1640. But always the Celt
was in the boy as a flute played over a hill.

The flute played but seldom after the boy's
guardian had taken over the farm, and there
followed long workdays in the furrows. It was
always the sons of the guardian who were
chosen to ride away on alluring errands to the
town; and when they did this, the boy heard
flute music and was impetuous to follow. But
his only contact with the world had been a
wagon-maker's invitation to an apprenticeship, abruptly terminated when the little un-
paid helper was cannily set to carrying bricks
for the wagon-maker's new house. Common
schools, farm labor, and this apprenticeship
— thus panoplied at nineteen the boy met the
open world.

He met the open world in Wisconsin, where
an older brother was a bridge-builder. About
the boy at this time lies that silence in which
are sealed the folk of fifty years ago. From
that pale amber rays one great gleam. The

arrival in a little Wisconsin town, its main
thoroughfare from the station but a half-mile
through a snowy grove. But station and grove
and town were hung with light: color of Asia
and the South Seas, of reef and peak and lamps
of London such as gilded all the pioneer places.
For the boy the wooden town offered a new
plane of energy and romance. A new aurora.

In Wisconsin in those days energy and romance centered in the railroad. Russell Sage's
fortune was contributing to stretch out inch
by inch the rails of the Chicago, Milwaukee
and St. Paul road — thirty-pound rails as
against the ninety-pound rails of the present,
but they were as great miracles as if they had
run there red-hot of their own power, and had
laid themselves westward for the traffic. Roar-
ing engines performed for the youth of the
day a considerable part of the function of
war, provided ready-made a point of release.
The bored, the maladjusted, the wistful, found
here a way of escape. A way, moreover, to adventure. Not everyone can trek his own trail
to reef or peak, but let there be beaten out any
highway toward glamour and feet are light
to set off. To the youths of the Middle West
in the sixties the locomotive was as a camel,
a howdah, a galleon, a griffin — plus, they
thought, excellent pay.

A brother-in-law of prevision offered college to the boy, but the boy had watched

the curve of the griffin's wing, and he
mounted.

There he was: slight, small-boned, pale, fas-
tidious. In the fine hair, delicate hands and
feet, light staccato step, above all in his grav-
ity, were met strains of Old World blood such
as united indifferently to turn the wheels of
the New World. Repeatedly you catch the
sign: on a frontier witness-stand, in a shop,
behind a plow, there will rise a profile or fall
a gesture out of Avalon. Emerging from his
blue denim collar, the boy's face, with the
appraising look of the reasonable, the sensitized, formed a cameo against the raw dark
of the locomotive cab.

Now came his days of first adventure:
strangeness, speed, risk, untoward hours. Feeding red the black mouth of the griffin through
days of wild cold, through nights on the snow-
plow thundering down the thick drifts. Danger and fear — and play, too. Lacking cricket
or curling, the boy played on the tender of the
moving engine, stooped to toss a stick of wood
at another youth, lost balance, and fell close
to the rolling wheels. He says: " As I fell, it
came to me to throw myself to one side, it
came to me suddenly. I did so — I fell so close
to the moving cars that I struck the ties and
sprained my foot, but there was no other in-
jury." When someone said: " But for your
presence of mind, you would have been ground

to pieces," he replied gravely: " But for that
— or something else," and this sense of inner
guidance was often with him. Every day there
was romance. Liberty from so many forms of
old routine, familiarity with night, hazard,
magic — fields for spirit and courage lay open
here as anywhere. The life held him. They gave
him an engine of his own and then they had
him fast.

But always from over the hill sounded the
flute. For him all these days of contingence
seemed but temporary. Inevitably there was
to be something other finally to occupy him
as life-in-earnest. Never was there any finality
of allegiance to the griffin. The boy went to
Missouri to look about, journeyed to the
Pennsylvania oil-fields. Vague aureate projects
formed and waited. And all the while the flute
kept calling to definite preparation against
that time: On his shelf three royal octavos of
Knight's Shakspere in a princely binding
of morocco and gold. On his wall a violin, and
he returning to his lodging, weary in body
and spirit from the sterile hours on a way
freight, still trudging off to a violin lesson.

He says: " I never expected to be a great
violinist. But violin music is the sweetest music
in the world — I thought so then and I think
so now."

And in his personal belongings there mani-
fested a scrupulous taste for silk — in those

days silk underthings were as rare as silver armor — and for delicate linen, hand-stitched, and for clothing "made to measure," as the little town accused.

The little town was growing now, unfolding petals of flimsy frame and thin blue glass. With the Civil War there came from the countryside new families whose men had gone to the war. And among them a family from New York State and a generation removed from England. In this family there were three daughters.

And now for the boy the flute poured in a thin tone an essence of Elsewhere. On Washington's birthday there was given in the town a ball, at which the boy danced in the same set of a quadrille with one of these three daughters. Under the mellow oil-lighting the costumes of the seventies touched and lifted upon the polished pine, pale Puritan and forgotten fabrics, silk mull, book-muslin, challis delaine, and sarsenet. The dances, definite, determined, occidental, were mazurka, money musk, varsovienne, the lanciers. Of these the boy remembers nothing save only that set of the lanciers in which he danced opposite to Her who "taught the torches to burn bright," and first touched her hand. But afterwards she herself could never recall the boy in the lanciers. One wonders what might have befallen had Juliet not recalled Romeo at the ball of the

Capulets. In that case Romeo, too, might not
have remembered. The boy may have been
greater than Romeo! For on no more than the
breathing presence of this lady the boy set his
faith, and for five years it did not waver.

He was twenty-nine. With gradual death
of the romance of the railway the mere habit
of his work took him for its own. And now
the new romance was enough. The vague aureate projects were dissolved in the incan-
descence of his noon. All day the flute was in
his ears.

It is with the cunning of the life principle
itself that a new country lures its pioneers.
Twice had he become the thrall of romance
— once of the road, now of nature. They called
it " securing a steady job on the railroad, mar-
rying and settling down." This was all that
their imagination could confine. What did
they know of griffins and flutes? And nothing
of the sovereign romance for the man in the
days that followed.

He had now a cottage reared almost literally
by his own hand, and there lived the lady of
the lanciers. There were a little child, a garden
with old fruit-trees and old roses and two
Lombardy poplars, a dog, and lyrical flights
of the griffin by day and by night.

For this time the contour should be double.
The lady of the lanciers had such beauty that
the neighboring towns knew her name; such

a voice that they came to her church to hear her sing in its choir. She could paint a little, play at the piano; and the cottage was kept by her own hand. Herself of pioneer stock and earlier of Sussex blood, she had a spirit and an independence to enliven the days and a common sense all but brilliant. She, the definite, the resolute, the humorous, bears a story of her own.[2]

They two shared a signal. Singing about her work or playing with the child under the apple-trees, she would hear across the east marshes a brief, abruptly silenced cry. To the others of the town this thin cry was no more than an engine whistle. But she would thrill as to a brazen trumpet. It was the horn of Siegfried winding from the valley, its motif a single silver note in exquisite restraint. Time to have delicious dishes on the table before he gained the house. Time to have the rooms lighted and to be waiting at a window with the baby. . . . Or at night waking alone in the cottage, hearing the child's nestling and the soft snapping of the blazing base-burner, watching the red outlines of shadow, she would hear cutting the dark that live, carrying call. He was coming. Exuberant romance this, undivined by followers of the tame vocations, but known to the wives of the road and of the sea.

[2] See "Eliza Beers," page 69

Yet always there was the terror: sullen nights of storm, of hardly averted fatality, of actual tragedy. Tales of a coach lifted on end in the dense snow and crashed upon the engine and of the five lives that went out in that gesture — five shovellers, whom the man and his crew laid aside decently as a part of the night's work. Of a midnight when the man ran down a farmer lying across the track like a body in a bag; and when an hour or two later a wanderer wounded in some fall tried to climb up to the man's cab, his young fireman, seeing that bleeding face at the window, cried out that it was the ghost of the dead farmer. And into the home yards that night the man brought his engine stoked by a fireman in lunacy. Five months later this fireman, a lad of twenty, died in his asylum cell.

And now for the man the flute began a new strain, touched with the plaintive, the perplexed. A strain about the future. If ill health came, death, what then of the lady of the lanciers and what of the child? At this the old bright projects glowed again.

Now had come the hour for the practice of an unpremeditated courage, courage of a heart still measuring youth. He left the railroad, left the town, went into a strange city. With a blindness which breeders of quail or of fish do not permit to a live thing that they wish to persist, the man took the way of the

hundred thousands who try to wrest a livelihood from a State unorganized to equip them
for the rudiments. Three times in three cities
in a period of twelve years the man sought a
way out through business. And three times he
returned to that which, save in imagination,
had never been anything but bondage. Ulysses
of three consecutive Odysseys, he fared. forth
with such initiative as America duplicates and
buries, sun by sun.

It is the years following the third return,
the years in which he had accepted the future
and had at last bowed to it, that should be
most intimately chronicled. Ill health was
threatening him now. The attempts to escape
had absorbed the greater part of his savings.
And there was the child to be educated — educated at college too; neither he nor his wife
ever questioned that.

Followed fifteen years of the old routine.

And life was supported with gentleness,
even with humor. A beautiful keen tenderness
was his for plants and animals, an oriental respect for life. They tell of him that on a summer night he caught up a kitten straying about
a railway station and gave it summary haven
within the open window of a ground-floor
room where it was instantly manifest that six
men had until then been sleeping on the floor.
As if this last burden were not to be sustained,
one moaned: " Here's Gale, putting a cat in

the window. . . ." Animals loved him. Walking to a strange farmhouse to ask for a direction, he was met in the dark by the farmer, who
demanded: " Yes, but how did you get by the
dog? She don't let a thing get past her. . . ."
The dog was trotting at the guest's heels. It
was as if animals knew that he served them.
Once he was going to his work when he passed
on the side track a car from which grain had
been unloaded. Among the scattered litter
from the sacks, the sparrows were having
breakfast. It was a frosty morning, and in its
eagerness one of the birds had stood too long
on the rail, and the little foot was held fast.
As the man approached, all the birds flew save
this one, which fluttered helplessly, its foot
fast on the frosty steel. So the man took off
his mitten, stooped, and held his hand on the
little foot till the warmth of his fingers released it, and the bird could fly. And once, in
a meadow, in deep summer, the man saw a
grass-snake moving in the green, and took up
a stone to kill it. He says: " Then I thought:
' What have you ever done to me? ' and I put
down the stone."

Plants would grow under his hand . . . a
stake which he set to mark a seedling rooted
and budded. It was in these days, after the
third return, that he developed a nostalgia —
it was nothing less — for country living; for
a farm such as the Ohio farm of his boyhood:

garden, orchard, brook, fields, a cow, a few sheep. Of these he rarely spoke, but always his wallet held clipped announcements of some little country place for sale, and he was never without a farm paper.

For years the man's free hours had been spent in second-hand book-stalls. There was always money for books: Spencer, Darwin, Emerson, Drummond, Bacon; through one winter he read Macaulay's *England* and then all of Fiske. He formed a habit of fathoming all words new to him in his reading, and by middle life had revised his vocabulary. An old taste for chemistry developed, and with a few scientific books he elicited enchantment. It was in a farm journal that he was attracted to a star map and peopled for himself the heavens. Creative thinking followed all his reading. He presented the theory, which he had never heard expounded, that the earth was never a molten mass cooling, but, instead, first of all, a world of waters whose deposit is the land. He questioned the methods of measuring the velocity of light; and years before there was any scientific dissatisfaction with the theory of the luminiferous ether, he had rebelled at that.

Politically he gradually became strongly liberal. A rich inheritance of liberalism was his. It was Henry Gale, his great grandfather, a Revolutionary soldier, who was a captain in

Shay's Rebellion, marched from Worcester to Springfield, to demand of the Supreme Court the repeal of the law for imprisonment for debt, was arrested, tried and condemned for treason, blindfolded, led out to be shot, and then reprieved. Now, on the town common at Springfield, Massachusetts, the " battle-place " where the regulars met the rebels, there stands in memory of that rebellion, a boulder with a copper plate, placed there by the Sons of the American Revolution!

And it was Abraham Gale, grandson of Richard, whose son Abijah, in 1773, was member of a committee appointed " to take into consideration ye rights as stated by ye Committee of Correspondence of ye town of Boston and of ye infringements and violations of ye same," and whose report, naming the grievances of the Colonies, adds: " For no dought ware tyranny is exercised, opposition becomes a duty. We cannot but look upon it as a hard Trial, yea, greater than we can bear, if we cannot be said to give full proof of our loyalty otherwise than by sacrificing those Rights and Liberties which we prize beyond life itself." And the man's allegiances were those of the spirit of the new day. He cannot remember when he did not favor equal suffrage. He cannot remember when he did not classify war as crime, and he has never spent a moment in regarding it as anything else. In religion he became nonconformist to nonconformists and all — profoundly religious, but aloof from any creed or group. The doctrine of forgiveness of sin and the abrogation of its consequences roused him to passionate scorn. Once he said: " And I have decided that Swedenborg wrote Revelation."

Thus he made for himself actualities to dominate, to displace those of the grinding days.

Withal he was ingeniously mechanical, clever at mending tools or machinery; would whisk out into a pie-tin the major works of a clock and return them to restored function, including chimes. His wood-house work-bench was completely equipped with carpenter's tools, all the repairing about the house was done by him, an occasional porch added by him, unassisted, and year after year the bird-houses which he made after a plan of his own were happily tenanted. All that he did was accomplished with a scrupulous, slow precision. His leisureliness extended itself to the table — of dyspepsia he had cured himself by Fletcherizing thirty years before Fletcher. He never hurried — the light staccato step had hardly slowed, his speech was deliberate when he spoke at all. He was a silent man. If he had been asked his favorite recreation, he would have said: " Home."

His preoccupations were seldom the particular. Because he had said that he had not

tasted prairie-chicken since he was a boy, someone brought him one, something of a feat in
a State in which the open season for these birds
lasts but three days a year. The prairie-chicken
was before him, the others were watching
eagerly for his delight, remembering as they
did that he had not tasted prairie-chicken
since he was a young boy and had himself
gone shooting. Everyone waited to hear what
he would say. And what he said was: "I see
that they are talking of forming a company
to handle the air mail. Those people will be
wanting to buy the post office next."

The solitary study, the long, lonely darkness on the engine, the daybreaks "gold and
wild," the countless expressionless days, had
crystallized an introspection always unique.
With no knowledge of the uses of contempla-
tion in the East, he acquired, and this quite
naturally, a habit of concentration, so that one
could enter a room or stand beside him in his
garden and find him unconscious of any presence. His time-slips, time-cards, stray enve-
lopes, and a note-book or two were covered
with notes made in the engine cab, at lunch-
counters, anywhere. These are a few trans-
criptions:

Our actions are our angels.

All laws are friendly to those who obey
them.

A new degree of intellectual power is cheap

The law of Nature is, Do the thing and you shall have the power, but they who do not shall not have the power.

The happiness of your life depends on the quality of your thoughts.

Children early catch the tone of their surroundings.

Most people are unhappy because they have no information concerning the real sources of enjoyment.

The guiding spirit. . . .

The details must be worked out with completeness to insure success. It is in this humble though all-conquering way that success is achieved.

Forget your grievances.

Until men grow up to the level of a higher life they cannot receive it.

Everything exists for something else of a higher order.

In your daily intercourse with men let your guiding principle be for the good of all.

Flashes of insight require systematic thought to unfold them.

Our thoughts materialize in our flesh and blood.

The child was now graduated from a university. For these four years of college training the man had paid on wages of three dollars and eighty-five cents for a trip (of ninety-odd miles), and meanwhile had maintained his home.

But always here the story bears the two outlines: one of his own patient, never robust figure faring to its toil; the other of the lady of the lanciers, of a resolution equal to his, rich in labor, sacrifice, thrift; herself individual, commanding, bearing her part in the life of the little town — and lovely. Two in a town of six thousand, and, so far as their influence might reach, the race safe in their hands.

Five years later temporary retirement became necessitated by ill health; and there were a garden, fruit-trees, unbroken leisure.

A total of forty-three years had been spent by the man on the railroad, all save the first two or three years in complete disillusion, in bondage. Out of this dissolution of the right to happy creative work there endured for him his wife, his child, and his home.

But what had been saved of the man's spirit, of his ambition to live, his love of fineness, the approaches to the social passion? Was he bitter, lethargic, in revolt? How had he himself appraised the quite unintentional tapestry of his life?

There was a record preserved in conversations, witness from the lips of the man; and he one of the men who ordinarily live and die in a community without the community divining the stupendous life which has been going on within. These comments, made in the last seven years, are more vivid than all else to yield up the man himself and the rich measure of his success in living.

It is now sixty years since, equipped with common school, a few years of farm work, and a brief apprenticeship to a wagon-maker, he fared through the snowy grove into the little frame town; seventy years since he faced the night sky drenched in the surging of the aurora. At seventy-nine here is the man, one of the brilliant potentialities by whom a less disjointed social life than our own might be how richly served.

(1)

I've had one of the days when nothing went right. It seemed as if everything tried to go wrong. And I thought how exactly that must be an example of the way the Spirit — or God — feels in trying to deal with us. He does the best he can, and we fail and retard him. He does the best he can and then comes war. I thought how discouraged the Spirit must be. Matter is obstinate. But it is all he has to express himself through.

(2)

[Over a new drain-pipe in the basement.] It is the way so many workmen work, with no thought of the trouble and expense to which they put other people. How can we expect them to know? With no training they go to their work, pick it up as best they can, and depend on it for the necessities of life. Their conscience is not trained. If, instead of pounding faith into them, we had developed their conscience, we should have a different set of beings. . . .

. . . Why should there not be, as well as a municipal fire department to put out fires after the damage is done, a municipal department to inspect private electric wiring and drains and water-pipes? They are beginning to do that for fire protection. But in all such work men should not be dependent on it for a livelihood. With these occupations on a commercial basis men do so often partake of the nature of the hog — of whose body their own body is so largely composed. All their lives they eat of the bodies of these animals, and certainly some of their nature passes over into those who consume them.

. . . For nineteen years, the first nineteen of my life, I ate no meat — perhaps a little tenderloin after butchering. The rest of the time I ate vegetables and bread. After I came to this town I learned to eat meat a little bit. I have watched men eat tough meat, a large piece in a few mouthfuls, almost without chewing. This seems to me the business of cannibals.

(3)

I've thought for years that immortality is
more simple and natural than we have realized.
That there is a close threefold relationship
in the air and the volatile part of our being
and God. We say that God is everywhere, and
we're not just sure what we mean. The immanence of God has been one of the puzzles;
the immanence of the air is some form we take
for granted. We have said that God is in all
life, and we haven't understood that either,
but we have spoken of the breath of life always. We have made a great mystery, but it
may be that this invisible substance which enters into all life as a spirit is close to the
mystery. There's nothing more materialistic in
that than in the admission that consciousness
functions through the brain. . . . After
death the volatile part of our being is released
and passes into the air — goes back into that
great reservoir of power, and seeks affinities
for reabsorption. And hence continuity. I
believe in such immortality because it is in
harmony with that which we see taking place
before our eyes every day. When we confine
immortality to a matter of the persistence
of the individual consciousness we limit our
inheritance.

(4)

I remember when that idea of immortality
first came to me with conviction. I was stand-

ing by a window looking at the river. And as I saw it flowing I thought: " Men come and men go but I go on forever." I thought how the river flows to the ocean, empties, returns to its source through clouds and moisture, becomes again a river, again flows. And that is exactly the way with spirit. It goes from us, it ceases to combine with the body and without it the body cannot live; spirit is reabsorbed into the spirit without, into the whole — we are in it all the time — we are floating in it — and it is reabsorbed in new living things. As an individual? No — that is impossible. When individuation has once been accomplished by spirit it is never lost; but it need not persist as one individuation. It will continue in many individuals. There is no more reason for insisting that the spirit of man is one eternally than for insisting that the spirit of God is one. God is not necessarily one intelligence. He is many intelligences. So of the spirit of man. For the spirit, in man and without, is a part of God. Whenever it can find the channel it speaks to us — to that of itself which is within us. To the divine in man. But the whole body is permeated with spirit — it is everywhere in the body. The air we breathe is spirit. It is the spirit of God. Without it we are only inanimate matter. At the instant it ceases to combine with us, we cease to exist.

Compare this with the doctrine of the soul

going off somewhere, to some place of heaven, and singing a psalm. Yet when they blundered into such an expression it was this immortality of spirit that they were seeking for. We are all blundering. But the whole process is so slow. It can only go on as spirit grows in the individual and is reabsorbed and grows again.

. . . Trees have intelligence. Spirit is combined with them in some degree, in their life and their intelligence. See how they seek out their food, find water, turn to the sun . . . there's a better explanation to this than the books make.

(5)

I don't think of God as law. I think of him as spirit. Law is his manifestation. I can conceive of his growing, but the law is static. It is simply a matter of finding out law. The law of evolution existed always, and at last the human understanding found it out, and so on. There are certain forces to which all things are subject, but things are acted upon differently by the same forces. A tree and a rock are both subject to gravitation, but the tree constantly lifts itself while a rock must remain in a fixed spot until it is destroyed. But different people are not acted upon differently by the same forces — people vary in perception and in response, that's all. The action of the forces toward them is the same.

(6)

As great a thinker as Herbert Spencer says
that he can see nowhere any evidence of design
in the universe. Others have said the same
thing. Nevertheless, there is everywhere evidence of design.

(7)

Man is slow in his development because he
does not pay attention to his intuitions. Now
and then there is one who is strong enough to
heed them, but most people let them go by,
are not strong enough to take them. The intuitions must be fostered for growth. One
form of these we call conscience. . . . As
these intuitions grow older and are developed
with each life lived they will be stronger to
speak. It is this part of living that matters.

(8)

(Some one had read aloud from Tagore's
Gitanjali: " Thou settest a barrier in thine own
being and then callest to thy severed selves
in myriad notes. This, thy self-separation, has
taken body in me.")

Yes. Nicolai, in *The Biology of War*, believes
and quotes others as believing that the universe is an organism. That is, that it consists
of one really organic whole, of which every
created thing is a member, as members of one
organism, one being.

(Comment: Then that organism would be God?)

The embodiment of God. And, as I believe, the " breath of life " is the divine essence of God, and constitutes the divine element entering into all life.

(9)

We are destined for the goal. And the goal is perfection. Sometimes we go on, sometimes we go back — but all the time the direction and destiny are the same: " Perfection." We reach one plane and another is above us. It is always the same. The time will come when the race will be an honor to God.

CHAPTER IV
Eliza Beers

I OPEN THE JOURNAL of my mother,[1] written
between the ages of fourteen and twenty-nine,
and thereafter having occasional entries until
shortly before her death, at seventy-six. And
from this journal, I divine that which books
unnumbered and priceless have been written
to witness, namely, that there is an inner order,
which a life may touch, become aware of and
thereafter express. Such expression in conduct,
these unnumbered and priceless books seem to
say, is the highest known form of creative art.
Both this theory and that of the behaviorists
I accept as the process by which there is beaten
into the race, into The Human Being, the slow
gold of his growth. If he can begin to be aware,
to carry on this growth consciously and with
a technique, so much the better. He has then
found the only short cut known to evolution,
in flowers, fruit, conduct and the like. If he
cannot be aware, Nature lets him be a be-
haviorist and will take care of him in spite of
himself.

My mother's journal documents her way of
awareness of an inner order, and her effort to
take part in such an order.

[1] Eliza Beers Gale, born October 31, 1846, Cuba, New York;
died May 29, 1923, Portage, Wisconsin. Daughter of Thomas Cook
Beers, born Pittsford, New York and of Harriet (Taylor) Beers,
born Rotherford, Sussex county, England.

One hundred and nineteen pages are all that she needed to record the reactions of twenty-seven years — of seventy-six years, if one counts those few entries of the fifty years when preparation had given place to participation. The slender green " marbled " volume, with red leather back and corners, holds thin fine faded words, inscribed with a delicate gold and pearl pen now in my possession. Begun in 1858 in New York State, continued in 1861 in Wisconsin and in 1872 in Minnesota, the book naïvely defines her own hour, names the cups from which she drank of life, and offers that taste of both the different and the unchanging, derivable from the forgotten and the reclaimed.

And then it is a moving thing to come upon so minute a record, written without self-consciousness by one without distinction save in her own group — and there she always had distinction. A pure form of self-expression this, intensely lyrical, recounted not by another but by the self. The stream of consciousness.

The first entry, July 21, 1861, written when she was fourteen, is this:

" July has almost gone and winter will soon be here, with its icy hand. I went to Sunday school and church, and after church went home with —. Oh, how thankful I should be if they would never enter our door again. It is well enough for them to come here once in a while, but they come every Sunday. I know it is wicked to indulge in such thoughts, but who can help it. I often think and so does my dear friend Sue, that it would have been better if we had never seen the boys. Little did we think at first that we would love them so. But Eliza, you had better stop. I see my mind has run too far. I do want a long, long talk with Sue. The world is cold and dark, and I groping my way in darkness. I wish I could do as the Lord says. Come unto me all ye that are weary and heavy-laden and I will give you rest. Oh, for that rest."

Here, at fourteen, is star dust for all the planetary movements of later years: Friendship, love, withdrawal, aspiration, despair, religion — and climate. A fortnight later:

" Today I feel as though I wanted to write something and I do not know what. I am lonely. What would I not give if Sue would come in and we could have one of our good long talks. I enjoy them so much. I feel I shall not always have her — we shall have to part, perhaps to far distant lands and perhaps by death. But am I prepared to meet my God? I fear not and I pray the Lord to help me in my weakness and strengthen my heart that I may live and bless his name."

I see my mother at twelve, arriving from her native New York State, with her mother, lately widowed, turning with her five children to her father's farm near Middleton Junction, not many miles from Madison, Wisconsin. But my mother's grandfather, Joseph Taylor, of Sussex, England, who with his sons had come to Wisconsin in 1849 and had taken up two hundred acres of government land, died while the family was en route to the west. They reached " the Junction " only to visit his grave and that of his wife, Constance Hoath Taylor, those two who had come from Rotherfield, near Tunbridge Wells, to the new world, where they had sought life and had found death.

The manner of that exodus from England has always thrilled me. They were small farmers, and were greatly annoyed by the riders to hounds dashing through their fields and garden, trampling down the growing things, a violation for which there was no redress. One night a cry went through the village that the smugglers were coming, riding up from the sea, at the mouth of the Rother river. Horses galloped through the village, there were the wagons of the smugglers and the officers in pursuit; and the smugglers began throwing down the smuggled goods, hoping to divert the attention of the law. But the officers shouted to the villagers to take the property into their houses, and continued the pursuit, returning next day, after the arrest of the marauders, to gather up the goods. But now the officers insisted on searching the houses of the Rotherfield folk, and they pushed by Joseph Taylor and his wife Constance, standing on their door-stone, with the cloths which they had collected from the cobbled street, and had held and were faithfully returning, and the officers entered their home and searched it. And it chanced that there was a bolt of new

cloth which Joseph Taylor had bought for
Constance to stitch for him some white shirts;
but the officers would not believe that this was
not a bolt of the smuggled goods, and they
seized it and took it away. This was too much
for the Taylors. Hounds and hunters they had
withstood, and Joseph had been " impressed "
into the army and had served at Gibraltar,
and had cut off the thumb of his own right
hand, so that he could not load a musket, rather
than go back into the colonial wars. But the
theft of this bolt of cloth was not to be borne.
Joseph and Constance and their five small children came to the new world, a six weeks' journey by sailing vessel. And for all their wrongs,
their preoccupation en route was perhaps
chiefly for a great meat " pasty " prepared for
the voyage and left on a cupboard shelf. I look
at the things that Constance brought with her
— the pitcher of " flowing blue," the Stafford-
shire sugar bowl, a cup of the first royal
Worcester made in England, the ten-sided
plate. I look at the graves of these two in the
Middleton cemetery. I read my mother's journal. The ache and the shine of the past are in
them all. On that farm, the Wisconsin harbor
of the Taylors, my mother's family remained;
a farm where stands today, erected by Joseph
Taylor and his sons, the barn of oaken hewn
timbers, now as hard as metal, still wearing the
wooden pegs and the marks of the adze, the

shingles of 1850, the great ancient hinges and the hasps. There too stands an apple tree, planted by Joseph Taylor, and yielding a fruit of smooth yellow, cheeked with rose — a giant tree, its middle eaten away, a sapling twelve feet high thrown up violently from the parent root, a tree nearly eighty years old, and still bearing its kind.

Here was Wisconsin in the decade follow-ings its admission as a state, when to it the in-flux to America had brought many Europeans, attracted by its easy residence requirement for citizenship. Here colonies of Swiss, of Dutch, of French were settling, but " the Junction " was a settlement of the English descended: the Sandfords, the Clewetts, the Gordons, the Smiths, the Slaughters, the Williamses — de-scended from Roger Williams — and the Tay-lors, seven families strong, comfortably housed, including one who began a great house which he was never able to finish. Sturdy, religious, thinking people they were, hard-working, lov-ing the land, content with little but ready for more. For social life there was church three times a day on Sunday, the worshippers plung-ing through drifts in winter, or, in summer, nibbling fresh caraway in the drowsy air. Their drama was the drama of family life, of birth, death, friendships, feuds. Their originality was unaware and unique: There was my mother's Uncle James, who conducted family prayers,

kneeling to petition for the liberation of the
slaves, and continuing the identical prayer for
years after the Emancipation Proclamation;
and there was my mother's Aunt Ephia Taylor,
who would never wear narrow skirts when
they came in style, but continued to wear full
skirts so that these could be cut over into bed
comforters. They had the pageantry of the
fields, they had choir music in the little white
church and the fresh young voices about the
cottage organs, they drove off behind medita-
tive bays and sorrels, in buggies, or in great
sleighs, belling their way to a chicken-pie supper or to a donation. It was at one such donation party at " the minister's " — where they
took the minister's wife a white dress " with a
sprig in it " — it was at such a party that
my mother and Flavia Camp met, the
mother of Dorothy Canfield Fisher, at home
from her school to visit her family at Black
Earth, the rich name of a village near " the
Junction."

Eliza Beers, at sixteen, was dark-skinned,
pink-cheeked, gray-eyed, black-haired, with a
contralto voice and a pretty wit and, in the
eastern fashion, skirts coming to her shoe-tops,
among the Junction girls whose skirts fell only
to the knees. The countryside soon knew of
the contralto voice. In the small white church,
close to the cross-roads, with caraway blowing
in the yard and a stile leading to the church-

yard, little Eliza Beers sang her way into many hearts. Once, in my little girlhood, I walked with her in a garden where caraway grew. She picked a spray, savored it, and said piercingly: " This used to grow round the Junction church." I hardly listened then, though now, when I pick caraway sometimes round that little church, still standing, I remember. That scent, that taste of caraway *which used to grow round the Junction church*. But when she said so, with her youth in her throat, no one cared.

" There is," she wrote (August 31, 1862), " a certain person that I love, yes, know that I love. Perhaps it is all folly, my placing my affections on him, but I can never forget him."

This was the little lad who had drawn her on his sled to school. Him I saw, at seventy, living in California, and he said to my mother: " I can see you yet, just as you looked when you came to the Junction church." And I heard them sing together, once more, " There's Music in the Air," and "How Sweet the Happy Evening's Close." They did not meet again.

My mother always detested the farm life. She was urban-minded, and her thought went back to her first home, a white house built by her father, Thomas Cook Beers, and still standing on the maple-shaded street in Cuba, Allegany county, New York, where she was born.

Her thought went back, too, to the long two-
day drives to her paternal grandfather's home
at Pittsford, New York, outside Rochester,
where there still stands, at the foot of Arm-
strong's Hill, having changed hands but once
in the one hundred and twenty years, the great
red brick house built by that grandfather, by
Edward Beers, about 1800, with its two hundred acres, its hawthorn hedges, its peach orchard, sugar bush and family burying ground.
And at the top of the hill there stood, within
my memory, the house built by her great-
grandfather, the Reverend Mr. Thomas Billinghurst, the first Baptist clergyman in the
county, whose portrait, done in oils, with his
wife, Ellen Brown Billinghurst, hangs still in
the little Baptist church at Pittsford. The sisters, Maria and Frances, were content enough
at " the Junction," and the brothers, Fred and
David, were busy with the farm. The mother,
Harriet Taylor Beers, always an invalid, was
bearing her share in the frontier life and already at forty-three was gray-haired and
lace-capped, and dreaming back to the log-
cabin, at Lyndon, New York, where her first
baby had been born — and she alone at the
time. But Eliza Beers was dreaming ahead.
When she had finished the district school, she
set out to find herself a school to teach, and at
fifteen appeared before her family with a first-
grade certificate and a school of her own, at

Pine Bluff, a dozen miles away. There, in a room twenty feet square, she taught fifty pupils, ranging in age from five to boys of eighteen, three years her senior. But she was tall and of dominant presence, with an English carriage and a certain austerity that never left her. When the five-year-olds fell asleep, she could be very tender; but when the " big boys " baited her with a difficult problem in algebra, she could go without lunch, spend the noon hour on the problem, triumphantly — but how casually! — explain it to the boys, and receive as slaves those young giants who, on the same problem, had driven out every previous teacher.

Nine dollars a month for a school year, and with this in pocket the young teacher announced that she was going to Madison to attend school. Not yet had the state university opened its doors to women, though the struggle had begun, and President Chadbourne was saying that if women were admitted to the University, he should resign. It is amusing to note that in forty-odd years, a woman's building at Wisconsin University was named Chadbourne hall; and that, although the university would have refused to admit Eliza Beers because she was a woman, her daughter became a trustee of the institution.

Eliza Beers and the Sue and the Anna of her Journal — her cousin Anna Taylor Noyes, and Susan Smith Goodwin — went to Madison, rented a room on the Capitol Square, and entered the Tullis Academy. This school was reminiscent of the Young Ladies' Select Seminary which little Eliza Beers had attended in Cuba, New York, when public schools were yet in bad odor. The Tullis Academy also was a school for young ladies, whose directors presided and slept through long hours dedicated to instruction — one of the schools opening here and there in those days of realization that the Middle West, too, might have its culture. Mathematics, English, deportment, history and orthography were the curriculum, and the families at " the Junction " took turns driving home the three students on Friday nights, and returned with them on Monday morning, bearing huge baskets; and were vastly indulgent of their daughters for whom the district school was not enough.

" I wanted to learn," Eliza Beers said, years later. " I wanted to know everything. I wanted to go into a bank — but nobody had ever heard of a woman in a bank."

Then came the Civil War. At " the Junction " this deviation from plow and harvest, from church and live-stock and market, found its welcome ready-made among the boys. There were meetings, recorded now as dry items under " Sixty-five years Ago " in Madison daily newspapers, but then beating and burning, as if every man there held his heart in his hands and hacked at it with a weapon, passioning for the slaves and against secessionists, for the unknown and against the Junction routine. Curiously, these days are almost unrecorded in my mother's journal — or perhaps not curiously, for she felt herself to be living now; and so wrote no more; but I have heard her tell of a Junction man who incited a hallfull of neighbors to enlist, and when they waited for him too to sign, said, " No, boys — it will kill father." There were the tents at Camp Randall, the visits there of Junction girls, vows, tintypes, and nights when boys leaped the fence, and walked the eight miles home, and were back again for *reveille*. Eliza Beers said good-bye to Chester, the boy beau who had drawn her on his sled, the " certain person " whom she loved. On that day in California I looked at the tintype of her and of " Sue," which he had carried throughout the war.

At " the Junction," Vicksburg and vows were one: " Will the war ever cease? " my mother wrote December 14, 1862. " It hangs like a dark cloud and why do I not have a letter from Chester."

Fred and David Beers enlisted, Eliza Beers came home from her school, and the family left the Taylor farm and moved down to " the Junction." As the war wore on, year after year,

and the times became more difficult, it was
necessary that Harriet Beers and her three
daughters go where they could earn. Also, the
eldest daughter had married, and her husband,
Jacob Learn, who was never to come back
from the war, had left her with a little son to
support. Their mode of choice of that new
home has often shaken me. Harriet Beers sat
before a map of Wisconsin and ran her finger
about upon towns.

" There," she said, " is Portage. I have heard
that Portage is a pleasant place to live."

On no more than this they chose Portage.
On no more than this, Eliza and Maria came
forty miles in a stage coach, taking two days
for the journey, the coach once over-turning
in the snow. On no more than this, one who
was so intimately concerned, myself, finds personal existence to depend. On my grand-
mother's finger, poised above a map and she
remembering a chance word about Portage,
spoken by whom? — a neighbor, a stranger,
perhaps a pedlar. Then that one, whoever he
was, went on his way unaware that a footless
shadow was clinging desperately to his spiritual
skirts, since it was in Portage, three years later,
that Eliza Beers met my father. My agitation
is natural when I read two entries in her
journal:

February 17, 1864. Here I am, away up in Portage.
(Portage is forty-four miles from " the Junction ")

Maria and I came here, rented a house, bought a stove, and expect the family next week.

December 30, 1866. Christmas has come and gone. I received a splendid album from Mr. Gale, a gentleman I have never spoken to.

My father had danced in the same set with her, in the lanciers, at a Good Templars' ball. But he had not met her and had been called away soon after; and returning toward Christmas he had sent her the gift, with a spirit direct and daring for those decorous days. The album, of tooled leather, lay on the parlor table in my childhood, lies in our home yet, filled with photographs of those days — including not only those from Portage, Wisconsin, but the Empress Carlotta and Maximilian, Moody and Sankey and General Tom Thumb.

When the Beers family had arrived, driven from Madison with their household goods by a Taylor uncle — this was years before the Madison railway line was built — the three daughters who were skilful with needle and scissors bought a fashion magazine, cut out the colored plates, hung them in the windows of their home and announced themselves ready to do dress-making and millinery. To such purpose did they work, the mother keeping the house, that when the two brothers, Fred and David, returned from the war, their soldier pay and their bounty — all of which, save one dollar a month, the boys had sent home! —

lay wrapped safe in the depths of a trunk awaiting them. There was no bank in Portage then, and when the drafts were taken to a local dry-goods store to be cashed, this favor was accorded only on condition that the applicant accept ten dollars in trade. . . . And still the total of the soldier pay had been kept intact. Fred and David. Two figures of 1865. There was a little ceremony when the money was presented, the women very proud and gay. David received his share and invested it in a book and music store in Portage; and the elder brother spent his in a single night at dissipation.

My mother had not lost her longing to finish school. She went to the Portage high school and entered. She was a ready student, delighting in mathematics, but English was my mother's bane. When the time came for the first theme writing, she appealed to a Middleton cousin, later one of the first women to graduate from Wisconsin university, the " Anna " of the journal, and asked her help in writing a " composition." Anna replied that she did not think this would be honest. So my mother gathered her books together and walked forlornly away from school. It was her last attempt to get " an education." I have thought that my own wistfulness to write may have been a secret compensatory urge because of that girl, walking down De Witt street with her books.

She was as far as ever from being a scholar or a banker; but preoccupations were many. She was the contralto singer in the Presbyterian choir, a choir which during the sermons sat and swung its handkerchiefs low over the floor, to warn away the mice. A youthful choir, seated under a rose window behind the minister, and laughing out one Sunday morning when he said: " Heaven is before me and Hell is behind me," and pointed, absentmindedly, in both directions. A choir whose melodeon used to lose a peg at critical moments in the anthem, when it was my mother's accepted duty to whirl, stoop, and replace it, without interrupting her part in the quartette; a small rosewood melodeon that now, sixty years later, stands as an innocent desk in the parsonage. There was singing too on summer evenings, the songs of war-time, " Bonny Heloise, the Belle of the Mohawk Vale," and " Rosalie, the Prairie Flower," and neighbors and passers-by gathered outside windows to listen. And on summer mornings my mother, and a girl with a clear soprano, a girl now dead for many years, would be driven forth at dawn by an urge that they did not define, and sitting on the open bridge across the Wisconsin river, they would sing together at sunrise and take the applause of the raftsmen drifting down the river with their logs of virgin pine. For winter evenings there were the dances and promenades — walking

promenades — of the Good Templars in Pettibone Hall, parties to which the county came,
even from so far as Johnston's Creek young
Ella Wheeler came — the Ella Wheeler Wilcox
of later days — entering the hall shyly in the
calf-skin shoes of the farm. There was the excitement of public protest against the scanda-
lous new dance, the waltz, — a group of Madison women were appealing to the Legislature
to stop these shocking exhibitions. When Pettibone Hall caught fire in the dead of night,
the whole town rose from its bed and ran
down the street; and these being the days before the volunteer fire departments, two long
lines were formed to the canal, and buckets
were handed — the full buckets by the men,
the empty by the women, among these my
mother. Pettibone Hall burned to the ground
notwithstanding, but the town never forgot
the thrill and the pageantry of that night. The
government canal, cutting the mile of the
Portage and following the Old Trail, which
Pere Marquette and Joliet and the John Jacob
Astor fur traders had taken, canoe on head,
from Fox river to Wisconsin river — that
canal has probably never more sincerely justi-
fied itself than on that night; nor will it so,
perhaps, until the St. Lawrence-to-the-Gulf
waterway flows through the little town, the
town that claimed five thousand inhabitants in
1865 and claims five thousand now.

By now my mother's journal bears this entry:

" September 15, 1867. Mr. Gale has been paying particular attention to me of late. Can it be that he is sincere? Do I love him? I shall wait until I am sure. He told me last Wednesday night that he had been pleased more and more with my company and would like it when convenient. He comes for me to go to church to-night. I suppose he is as fine a young man as there is in town."

Through the winter of 1867, which she spent in New York state, this fine young man is much in her thought. October 20 she writes:

" I had a very singular dream last night. I dreamed that Charlie (Mr. Gale) proposed to me.

II

It is in the entries throughout this winter in New York, as in the entries of those earliest Middleton days, not more than in the days of the courageous Portage years, that the deeply religious note in the nature of this light-hearted young girl expressed itself. That note which I have called the recognition of an inner order and the urge to join in its operations. As I read, it seems to me that these expressions are less inheritance, less the Presbyterian, or any other influence than, shall one say, chemical — a kind of chemistry beyond the spiritual, beyond the emotional. It is as if she had within her elements that could combine in some great planetary chemical change which she divined, without being aware of. There was, to be sure, also the explicable religious yearning. At eighteen an engagement had been broken, and she wrote:

" If I could only cast my burden on the Lord. How I have prayed that I might be at rest. I feel like exclaiming with the poet, The light of heaven to regain, alas, how difficult. Teach me, Lord."

There had run on the recital of vows to love always, of partings immediately after, of re-unions, and then of final separation, and in the midst of all:

" Shall I ever be a Christian. I pray God that I may. Help me, Lord, to love and serve thee. I sometimes think Jesus does love me. I shall try after this to serve him and by the grace of God I shall succeed."

But months later she writes:

" Oh, how long have I been searching for Jesus. Now I feel I have found him. How it came I cannot tell. But I prayed for light and it dawned on me."

She has told me that after weeks of a sense of burden, weeks filled with prayer, she was descending the stairs at her home when it was as if a voice said to her: " My strength is suffi-cient for thee." She said that there came to her then the realization that she need not find re-lease herself, but that she need only claim it; and this was followed by the usual phenomena of relief and joy. She united with the

Presbyterian Church and was accustomed to relate: " And I have never been so angry in my life as I was that afternoon." This never ceased to cause her sadness.

From New York she writes:

I have been deprived of church privileges very much, since I have been here. Do I live as becomes a child of God. I have given myself to Christ for time and eternity. After making the vows I have, should I go back into the world and forget, as I have often done, my obligation to the glory of God. Should I become pleased with the trifles and pursue like the worldling the vain things of this life. But how shall a fickle treacherous heart like mine be kept from wandering. How shall I ever be able to keep the solemn covenant I have entered into. It can only be through him whose strength is made perfect through weakness. And I do hope that by his assistance, I shall be able to live more to the glory of God than I have done. Blessed God, fill my mind with thy glorious perfection."

On New Year's day of 1868, there is entered the following:

" Tremble, O my soul, at the review of the past year. Think of the faults that have rapidly accumulated during one short year. O Lord, cover me with a robe of righteousness that my misimproved years may not rise up in judgment against me. Examine, O my soul, the foundation of the hope to which thou art still clinging. Remember, there is a hope that perishes. O may my hope not be of this kind. May I strive to do better this year. May I love the Lord with all my strength and my neighbor as myself. . . . Went for a cutter ride this afternoon which I enjoyed very much."

A girl of twenty-two, filled with joy of life, of music, of adventure, tribal in the extreme, romantic and with abundant food for romance, cannot be said to turn to religion because of isolation, loneliness, lack of active life, driving her to turn to real or imaginary spiritual experience. The explanation of abounding creative life, seeking outlets where it might, in romance, in religion, is less interesting and less final, and to me, knowing her later life, less probable, than a far simpler interpretation. For given the stimulus of aspiration, she seems to have realized that aspiration is not enough, and to have been seeking a technique.

On her return from New York in April, 1868, the circumstance of her engagement to my father deepened her search for ' the good life.'

" Next to my Creator, Charlie. Is there any such thing as loving one too much. O there cannot be. My prayer is that I may continue to love God most and Charlie next. Keep me from having my treasure on earth, but in heaven."

" I think of him so much and have so many happy thoughts of our future. *Our future* — how queer that sounds. Over a month since we were engaged and the love seems to grow upon me."

" God forbid that I should ever think less of him. And when I think that we are both trying to serve one God, how much happiness it gives me. He is so good. May I prove a true and loving wife. Deep unutterable joy. . . . I must just accept it all and love God and everyone more than ever.

A week after their marriage, four years later, she writes from Minnesota:

" If the rest of my life I can be as happy as I have been thus far, I shall have no cause of complaint, and not for all the wealth of the worlds would I go back where I was."

" O Lord, wilt thou guide me and direct me. Keep me that I may be a living example of what a Christian should be. Help me to see clearly. Put words of wisdom in my mouth. I can do nothing without thy aid."

" O God grant that I may see my first plans in married life, my first hopes, include a true love to God and a true purpose in serving him. It will not be enough that I love my husband. He must be my head in the Lord. He must interpret to me God's love. But he is not God. If I hope in any besides God, my ladder will be on the ground, but too short to reach farther than the storm clouds and ere long the wind will blow it down. Nothing is so beautiful as the temple that love builds. O may our house be built of love. It must be God in me that shall maintain me in that dignity and nobility which shall hold *his* love. . . . Make me pure, Lord, and fill my heart with godliness. . . .

There is in the volume not an entry of any length which does not center about this urge for perfection in life and love. From the first expressions of her little girl-hood — " I pray the Lord to help me in my weakness and to strengthen my heart " — on to that lyric utterance: " Nothing is so beautiful as the temple that love builds. O may our house be built of love " — the whole record speaks an awareness of an inner order, an aspiration to combine with it, and a search for a technique in that delicate progress. Her reaction to most of experience bears evidence of this uninterrupted awareness of its spiritual interpretation, and of constant seeking to deepen that awareness. She writes:

" One of God's most beautiful days. How good he is to us and how little I do for him."

" What a beautiful night, the moon shedding its pale light down on the earth while frost glimmers from every branch and twig. Beautiful world, and do we appreciate as we should. Do we return thanks to the giver of all good for this beauty. How much we have to thank him for — pleasant home, friends, the Bible — oh, how little I do for him in return."

She sings at a concert in Madison, and " was spoken of very highly," and continues:

" I thank God he has given me my voice. May I use it to his glory."

There are two mob lynchings in Portage in September 1869. She records the events and that which led up to them, and ends:

" What are the people thinking of? Vengeance is mine, I will repay, saith the Lord."

In other ways besides in the impulse to be articulate in the journal, she had a creative urge. She had not a dozen music lessons, but she mastered the organ and melodeon sufficiently to play for the church singing at times, and she had some skill at the piano. Her voice was her greatest means of expression, and she sang and played her own accompaniments all her life, the rich tones persisting until long past middle life. She studied painting in oils: " I have finished another painting — a scene on the Rhine." " I have painted a pastoral scene." " I have painted Goodrich Castle, England." This castle hangs now in my room, simple and direct, like an English primitive, and almost modern. She was much in demand at " private theatricals," that early mother of the Little Theater movement, — I recall her in jet, singing in " Lost and Saved," at the Portage Opera House. The poetry which found its way to her she read eagerly: Miss Muloch, Bayard Taylor, Thomas Moore. She copies out a poem of Moore's and prefaces it:

" Do I deserve this happiness? God knows I do not — why is it I am so cold in his service? Help me, gracious Lord, that I may be more faithful, help us *both* that we may be found ever ready to work for Thee, and Heavenly Father, wilt Thou watch him and guard him. . . . I shall try to look on the bright side, but if anything should happen that I should never be with him, what would I be without him.

> ' How sweetly does the moonlight smile
> Tonight on yonder leafy isle.
> Oft in my fancy's wandering
> I've wished that little isle had wings,
> And we within its fairy bowers
> Were wafted off to seas unknown,
> Where not a pulse would beat but ours
> And we might live and die alone.' "

Her aspiration and a search for a technique for its expression in conduct never ceases. Two years after marriage she writes:

" It seems as if the love grows stronger every day of my life. Do I love him too much? Surely not, for did not the good Father so constitute us that we are to love. . . . Bless us, heavenly Father, in our love for each other, and in that love may we not forget that all these earthly blessings come from Thee."

Following my birth, every entry has to do with the responsibility felt by her — " may I teach her so to live . . ." and " Can I bring her up as He would have me." But there is no entry of that which she has told me, that in the months of waiting my arrival, countless times daily she would leave the room, where she sat sewing with her mother and sisters, and would pray, not for her safety or mine, but for the usefulness of the young life that she awaited. " I was possessed to pray for this," she would say.

From 1876 to 1889 there is no entry, but when one is made, these thirteen years have not breathed upon the bloom of her desire. The entry is intimate, the religious note is the same. She adds:

" This is the last I shall write. I shall copy here some of my daughter's poems, for she has developed a talent for writing."

— and I am interested to note, in those uncommonly bad contributions, their inevitably

religious cast. The first page of quatrains, after
one about a millinery shop written at six years,
" The Soul," is written at thirteen. I mention this because I do not feel that the religious
atmosphere of her daughter's upbringing was
alone responsible for this choice, but rather
something other — shall we say something
chemical? — communicated by the mother. I
do not mean by her body, before the birth she
awaited, but by the totality of her presence. I
do not use scientific, or pseudo-scientific
terms for this effect, for it is something other,
which we may know more about or may dis-
card, as time suggests.

Twenty-eight years later Eliza Beers writes:
" What can I say of my past life? I have
tried so hard to do right."

And then this sentence, as from a saga:
" It is wonderful to look back over my life,
and to see the changes."

She recounts the friends who have gone, and
now, at seventy, she says:
" Where, where are they? Will I ever see
them again. Yes, I believe."

In the final entry, January 1920:

" O, I have tried so hard to be a good wife and mother.
I do not know if I have succeeded, but I do know that
I love them both with an everlasting love. Help us, Lord,
to believe. . . ."

It is necessary to have in mind that all who
have known her have known first of all a

laughing, fun-loving, mischievous, and popular girl, albeit with a dignity upon her from her earliest years; and then a young woman of beauty and charm and gaiety, the number of whose suitors was the despair of her mother. And I myself have known her as a woman of joyous humor, a delicious wit, a happy attitude toward every circumstance of her life; as one who, to her last day, was the spirit of every party and who, literally in her last hours, jested with us all. She had great magnetism, and her face was always as if illumined from within.

Here was no religion that " found God and turned plain." Here was a religion that lighted a lamp in a vessel. Here was a nature that, on the food of formal religion, loved and served God, did divine an inner order in the universe, did attempt all her life to bring herself into harmony with it and, or so it seemed to us who looked on, did succeed.

CHAPTER V
The United States and the Artist

ONE'S FIRST LIGHT THOUGHT was: "What United States? New York — or the Middle West — or Pasadena. It must be difficult for an artist to function in New York, with so few hours and so much food — or so little; and still more difficult in California, with all the scenery and the leisure. If I were an artist in the United States, I should work in the Middle West, with dashes to New York for brief vacations (not for stimulus) and with occasional golden dragging days across the desert, to establish a relationship with space. And when I came home again, from either direction, my town would say: " I suppose you go away to get points, and come back and write them up? "

It should be a small Middle Western town — it should be Portage, Wisconsin — with a lawn running down to a river, a river intent, not to say distrait. On the other shore there should be only green, with a far brow of hills: At noon one could go out and lie in the sun, and stay there through the whole afternoon. If winter came, the lawn and the farther shore would be white, and the whiteness would not darken; and one's window would have a long chair and a primrose.

Nothing would happen. Morning would be four hours long, sunny or in the ancient expressionism of cloudy light. A squirrel, the Westminster clock, a chickadee or a grosbeak, and the wheels or the runners under a passing load of straw would offer the principal sounds. Afternoon would end *when it chose*, in a walk across the river, the " levy " and the open fields being not at a ten-minute distance, and the white or green intimately at hand. The evening would be for reading or for writing or for friends. All the days would be the same. One wouldn't be invited to lunch, because one doesn't play bridge. One wouldn't be invited to dinner, because one isn't married. One's evening would be intact because one doesn't dance. But an intimate touch with the town would be held in other ways — by school, park, library, and many a hearth. Above all, by children.

Can an artist exist and function freely in the United States? I think that he can do so if he knows where and how.

Unless he falls upon a place or a period of cliques, extolling new nonconformities and their resulting classification, the artist leads among men the loneliest life of them all. This he must do, because his work is as solitary as being born — more so, when you come to think of it. And it is true that in whatever country he works, even in one long ridden by

prejudice and standardization, his four walls
and his tools are all that he needs — during his
actual hours of creation; and that in the ripest
nation as in the most callow, while he is
at work, the artist is independent of the
State. But it is when he emerges from that
room and becomes again a social being that
he sighs to think — if he does — of the dis-
abilities of his country as a garden for his
growth. It is then that he fears its effect —
if he does fear — upon his exalted hours of
creation.

A former sigh for the lack of adequate criticism he need no longer breathe. Synthetic
criticism arrived among us abruptly. The last
ten years, having seen the rise of the liberal
weeklies and reviews, have welcomed the rise
of a critical estimate as high and free for literature, including drama, as for government, including the pageant of politics. Careful criticism of music and painting was known in the
United States much earlier than was significant
literary criticism. The proportion of critical
work to the totality of mere review work is
still approximately that of the new pyramidal
architecture of Manhattan to its old expressionless acreage of brick and brown stone; but
of such cardinal criticism there is a surprising
weekly amount, and it is a momentous part of
our new national life in art. The growth in
general art-criticism is provable not only in

New York and Chicago, but in the newspapers of Detroit, Cleveland, St. Louis, St. Paul, and in the fascinating bulletins of print-shops, book departments, and non-professional dramatic groups in Minneapolis, Milwaukee, and the Far West. There are writers putting out such subtle and synthetic comment as a dozen years ago was quite unknown to us, outside the established reviews; or inside either. To what nation shall we turn, however, in which an accurate estimate can be promised to all artists; and what have even the mellow nations not done to both the little artists and the giants? There may be an inclination to abuse as national an international custom.

A modern international tendency to revalue prize-offers and even "learned societies" is saving the artist of this country regret that his land goes in so gingerly for both. The artist is in a mood to criticize the efficacy of prizes, and to say that these are to art what the Golden Rule is to conduct — something for a people to outgrow in favor of the thing itself. Likewise he questions the function of the older art-organizations — boldly if he is a pictorial or a plastic artist; shyly, for some reason, if he is an artist in literature. For such lusters and elevations the American artist might have longed a half-century ago, but now, having made out without them, he openly challenges them in both Old World and New. But pensions and their like the artist of either world may regard wistfully, especially on being admonished: " Go out and prove that you can earn your living with your hands, and *then* you'll have the right to be an artist."

I am unable to believe that the United States is flawed for the creative worker by that which may be called a Constitutional taint. In a land in which all men are created equal, there are yet many whom one can be perfectly sure are wiser than oneself. The search for mental superiors to rub up against is assuredly rewarded, for in every town are beings ripe, wise, international in their literary and musical loves; and these, created equal though they may have been, have become undeniably and even unpatriotically more interesting and more stimulating than their fellows. I do not speak, of course, of the privileged as such, but of the great and simple. There is in the United States a growing body of those in whom Henry Adams might have found delight and with whom, time having passed since his time, he might now adventure toward his spiritual inconclusions. It may be charged that the American scene abounds in those who are neither great nor simple; but even the English artist of humor has some uncongeniality to meet. For such a name — to improvise — as Araminta Throgmorton is not humorous in London. And once a celebrated British critic cried, apropos of free verse: " If this goes on, what is to become of the iambic pentameter? "

Certain hazards among us, then, are to be conceded and survived. Others there are, and if the artist is a Negro, his difficulties are needlessly greater in this country than in any other land in the civilized world. In general the great United States handicap is none of these. It lies deeper and is not to be conquered by praise or fellowship or loaf and flask. It is that which we know well, that whose despair is in the very form of the query. It is the lack in the national life of that indefinable control by the ordered, the accustomed, the mellow, the dreaming, the old. For there can be no doubt that we have of these nothing to enjoy that is at all commensurate with our wistfulness. That rhythm, that murmur, that balanced movement which is confident but not complacent, which is exquisitely practiced and withal a little weary — we have not its moderations nor its measures. In one hour of Rome or of Chartres, before proportion, relationship, serenity, equilibrium, we follow the line that goes straight from the human spirit to its evocation in art; and thereupon an image of our industrial cities or of our frontier towns becomes a weariness. We know that we are without our memories or our echoes. Time is neither our asset nor our despair, but merely our hope. We are not the Old World.

We are not the Old World. But yet this cannot be called precisely the condition from which, in order to function creatively, we are seeking to recover. The memory of the *Mayflower* must have been, at moments, a weariness to the Pilgrims who had chosen her. Still, on completing a meeting-house in the woods none did inquire: " Where is the nave and where the transept? " Nor did one of them step upon Cape Cod or Plymouth Rock and observe: " This place appears to lack the austerity of the tombs in the Abbey." Or, if anybody did, we shall never know it, for the Fathers dispensed with him, into the deep. They had come in search of liberty of expression and not to mourn old power or beauty. They had come to express themselves *in a life which had yet to be born;* which is still being born, when traditionalists and fundamentalists will keep out of the way. Unluckily no effective revolutionists in art accompanied the Pilgrims. We had to wait for Whitman to begin that nascency; but since Whitman it has not been so leisurely a business. Now we face in our native art a moment comparable to that of 1776 and after. And who was there in 1776 and after who was saying: " Yes, aristocracy best fosters us. We have made our experiment; we have proved that England is more mellow than the colonies. We wish to be mellow "?

Now, in 1928, we are still committed to our

experiment. And it was not made of political and religious bread alone. Laboratories in faith and in government have added unto themselves laboratories in social theory, in industrialism, in science, in behavior. And quietly our art is arising. Art is not a department by itself. Art is the imaginative interpretation of the life of a people, *whatever that life may be.*

If I were an artist, I should, in the light of my experience, stay at home and confidently expect to do my work. I should know that from out the decays of Italy and the fatigues of France and the deepening impassivities of Great Britain one could look, and imagine no more challenging artistic adventure than waits in this land with the unimaginative name. (Perhaps our name is our only artistic handicap. Perhaps if we had for ourselves the lovely word " America," or if we were called Columbia, we should already be acquiring a fragrance as of our burnt umber harvests.) I should know that if in the ancient days I had gone questing for a field, I should very likely have renounced everything in exchange for the terms of our unique life. Our breathless North American industrial towns, plump suburbs, motionless farms, preoccupied mountains; our desert, either as pure color today or as seed of the cities of tomorrow; and our little towns, faintly figuring the velvet of their vast fields, white or green — these are not mere material for art; these are stuff of the life of art. That definition is a repetend for our thinking: art is the imaginative interpretation of the life of the people, *whatever that life may be*.

Art is more than this. Art seeks to interpret the human spirit, naked in the universe, itself without nationality or academy or learned society or pension or past. The chief claim to be an artist which any artist has is his incurable gift of discerning that lovely laboring progress of the spirit. If, then, an artist looks out upon that spirit hard enough, even in this land so lacking in the scrutiny, the pattern, or the label of the past, albeit not without something of the fragrance of the universal breath, it may be that he will forget the difficulties of keeping his covenant in the United States.

He will be in no illusion. He will know, sadly enough, that he has turned from the flowered debris, the resonant footsteps, the delicate somnolence, the emanations of genius and of ruin. He will be in no illusion. And when our one hundred percenters come and tell him that he has the best country on earth to write in, he will emphatically demur. He will reply that there is no best country to write in. There are only an Old World and a New. You make your choice.

CHAPTER VI

Implications

TWO RIVERS FLOW toward Portage, Wisconsin, and succeed in meeting, save for a mile's distance. Between the Fox, flowing northwards, and the Wisconsin, flowing towards the south, this mile became the portage across which, in Astor fur-trading days, Indians and the French, including Joliet and Père Marquette, carried their canoes on their heads. Now a government canal connects the two rivers, and the water-spirits of the two rivers find themselves of one race. And over the little town, of an expectant early morning or of a tiptoe noon, one catches a clear horn from launch or from motor boat, signaling to the lock-master to open the locks and to let the waters meet.

It is that signal which gives one pause. For they do not make it with a whistle or a horn. All the small river-craft carry a conch shell. Knocking about the bottom of the boat the conch shell will lie, and on its opened end will be blown the blast, monotonous and silvery. One wonders where they find these shells, for one recollects them in one's childhood as inhabiting parlor floors exclusively, and one doesn't know how they escaped into boats. But there they lie, there they are lifted and sounded. And the latency is this: that not to one in many of those who are boating, and who signal by the shell, and not to one in many of those who from the shore hear that sweet metallic summons, is it known that the custom echoes the life and habits of a god of Greek myth, of Triton, whose custom it was to rise from the waves of the loud-sounding sea, and blow his wreathed horn.

It is related that a visitor to the Cornish coast noted the evening routine of the mussel-gatherers, who, when the tide begins to come in, rise, cup mouth in hands, and shout a warning up-coast, to the other mussel-gatherers. And that shrill and warning cry consists of one word — the word " Æger," shouted and repeated up those rocky ways. The visitor asked one of these mussel-gatherers why he cried that word, and received the expressionless reply that the tide was coming in. Yes, but why did he cry out that word? The man didn't know. No mussel-gatherer knew. And the stranger, being curious, sought out the word, and found it to be an old Celtic name for water-god.

Mr. Lewis Browne in *This Believing World* instances the primitive belief that at death the released spirit became hostile to the beloved ones left on earth. So, if his family was black, they painted their bodies white, and if they were white, they painted their bodies black, so that they might be invisible to those inimical spirits of the dead. And thus our most elegant mourning gown, or stationery, or that slight black arm-band are survivals in us, having white bodies, of the days when white bodies were painted black for the protection of invisibility from the dead.

I remember seeing in my childhood an illustration of a " heathen idol," which a class was told was a hideous monster, because it had many hands and many faces. But the comment of a brahmin was " Ah yes, the all-seeing one, the all-powerful one, represented with the many hands and eyes."

One might multiply these implications, as Frazier does, in *The Golden Bough*. Implications to which few attend, standing mutely, as they do, deeply among our accepted interpretations, among our habits and conventions. But the romance, the true interpretation of any habit, of any convention, lies in this faint inner significance for which few have memory or attention. It is to the discovery of this implication in history and in biography that we owe the new history, the new biography, begun in our time. We name this now the humanizing of biography, of history, of knowledge, but this means the discovery of implications long nonchalantly regarded, if regarded at all.

The neglected implications of daily human living, when at last these are observed, move us most. There is a house where sits all day by a window a woman in the eighties, saying:

"There goes Blank. That's the second time she has been downtown today."

"There goes Blank. She'd better take an umbrella. That's her best suit."

"Look at him. Got a tin pail. Must be going for buttermilk. I wonder what his wife is going to make."

"Look at her. Going pell-mell downtown. There she goes back. Likely she forgot her sample."

This goes on by the hour. And the family is frankly bored. "What," they say, "makes mother do that all day?" But one member of the family was pierced at last by the reason that mother did so. Here was a woman whose life had been filled with action and event, who had been accustomed to participate in all that went on about her. Now in late life, old and ill, she was no longer able to play her part. This window occupation was her manner of co-operating still, of pretending to some little rôle of participation. Instead of a garrulous on-looker, she was thus divined to be a tragic figure, the immemorial being of life and action fallen upon its days of idleness.

One sees a woman of advanced years enter a café a moment before her companion. The waiters are obviously surprised to see the older woman enter alone — she has that strange hesitation and misdirection which attacks the aged. They seat her, and their concern is not defer-

ence, but a compassion, which she must feel,
without ever having grown accustomed to feeling. For as soon as she is joined by her companion, a young woman in the thirties who gives
the order, the older woman begins to say:
" And have the plates hot — have them very
hot. And have them make my tea in a hot pot
— have them heat the pot well before they
pour in the hot water. And when they poach
my egg, don't let them have the water boiling
. . ." and so on. The waiter is amused, the
companion is annoyed, and neither under-
stands that the old lady, helped and pitied and
set aside, is building up a defense of importance. If one were writing about her, the old
lady whom the waiters and the companion saw
would be a boring and stupid figure, but all
the time there would be the other old lady, trying to recapture a position forever lost to her,
a tragic and eternal figure. A youngish man
enters a restaurant, for breakfast, and asks for
a grapefruit. " Don't cut it," he says, " bring
it to me whole." A few moments later he is
heard accusing excitedly: " You have cut the
grapefruit. I told you to bring it to me whole.
Take it back. Bring it to me as God made it."
An authentic fancy perhaps, on his part, but
the one who wrote about him as merely irri-
table would miss the man. Once, only Balzac
and his kind would have seen the little figure
laboriously building up for his own enjoyment

that sense of his own consequence; but now the new psychology has exposed the writer's divination, and anyone at any table may read that grapefruit instance for what it is — and not to despise, but to understand, to see a little deeper into the nature of the being.

In *Show Boat* Edna Ferber sets a sentence which lit for me a forgotten and misinterpreted girl of my school-days. To this young woman everything was a crisis. The loss of a book, a failure to keep an appointment, to receive a telephone message, to mail a letter, became a crisis, shrilly described. One used to be amused by it, then impatient. Edna Ferber's character is asked whether such an one, being ill, had a nurse, and, given in Mississippi days when such attendance was rare, the reply runs: " Of course. She has too strong a sense of the dramatic not to have a nurse when she is ill." So I saw at last what was the matter with Maude, of the incessantly manufactured crises.

If you write about any of these people as they probably seem to the family, to the on-looker, you have automata. Boatman, mussel-gatherer, mourner, and " heathen idol "; old woman at the window, old woman or young man in the café, woman with a nurse, girl emphasizing every trifle, teacher or parent exercising the romance of authority — all these, being merely recorded, are no more than surfaces. But any one of these interpreted, his actions touched with their own secret relationships, becomes at once a figure of another importance, a figure on altogether another scale of significance.

The unexpressed is of immeasurably greater value than the expressed. Not only has the human being a more vital import than the aspect which he presents to us, which already we know if we know anything of the race, but we are in danger of missing him altogether if somebody does not interpret even the aspect with which we think that we are " familiar." Once, only the Balzacs could do this — and then we thought that they wrote of unique instances. Now the new psychology can make Balzacs of observation of us all. All that we lack is expression!

This marks an immense advance in the treatment of fiction material. It is not less than the discovery of one of the three great secrets. The secret of the urge to write at all is inviolable; the secret of style is, after all, the mystery of the clothing of a flower; but the secret of the understanding of human beings is now something in which all the world may share. A dismaying number of people are, by this broad door, already entered upon fiction-writing. They not unnaturally feel this magic to be enough. It is not enough, but its revelation is doing its great bit toward the ostracism from literature of machine-made characters.

In the inevitable reaction of literature upon life we thus proceed to enrich life by undivined implications. A child looks out the window and says: " There comes my snow," and we see the arrogant individualism of childhood. Playing up to this individualism, a mother says: " See the man, making a path for Maizie," and hears Maizie say: " Man making a path for all peoples," and the mother sees the dawn of group consciousness in the child. Little Peggy asks: " Why should you be good, anyway? " — and hears something about growth, or even design, and cries vigorously: " Is *that* the reason? Well, people don't know that. *I'm going to tell people*," and with a far look calculates: " I could tell a hundred," and there is in the small face an evangelical fire. Little Lucile is said to laugh at silly things, and defends herself: " I saw my feet go back and forth from my skirt and they looked so funny " — and you discern in the child an ability to isolate the familiar and to seize on the humor of the hackneyed. These implications make all the difference between the open book and the closed covers of a personality.

It is a commonplace that in the best stories the humor lies in the implication. As in that shortest ghost-story ever written, of the two meeting in the picture-gallery of a haunted house. The first comer asked: " Aren't you afraid of the ghost? " The new-comer ex-

claimed: " No! I don't believe in ghosts."
Whereupon the other observed: " Oh, don't
you? " — and vanished. It is a commonplace
that in the most dramatic moments of a play
the implication carries all. Great drama *is* great
implication. It seems certain that in implication lies all acute understanding of the human
scene, all fine characterization of its figures.
The line between great fiction and little fiction
lies in the implication as detected or as unde-
tected by the writer.

Supremacy in importance among recent
tendencies in fiction goes therefore to that
now generally conditioning the new fiction;
namely, the isolating and interpreting of the
material between the lines.

CHAPTER VII
Conversation

THE CELEBRATED AUTHOR SAID: " I know what's the matter with the book. Until the final moment it concerns itself with reality. In the last three pages it lets go of the known and leaps at the unknown. You feel cheated. You've trusted to facts and you're delivered to speculation."

She answered: " In a day of routine, which would you call memorable — the routine or the occasional inexplicable moment? "

" That's nothing to do with art."

" Life hasn't? "

" Not all of life, of course. Obviously art is selective or it is nothing. Hear this forever: Life has to do with the ascertainable."

" The ascertainable by whom? "

" Why — by the artist."

" Precisely. By the creative artist. More life will be ascertainable by him than by those who deal exclusively with the physical. To the agent, the artist's commonplace will be the unascertainable."

" There's a common field for them all. That is the field of art. The technique is not in that common field, since technique must be known only to the specialist. But its effects must be open to everybody. Implications will depend on the sensitivity of the reader — but the sub-ject-matter itself — the material for art — must consist of nothing but the known."

"Known to whom?"

The Celebrated Artist was impatient at this rude insistence. "Look here — a fragment of a dead Greek poet, unnamed — a frag-ment about bright frocks in a meadow on a holiday — I'd give more for that than for all your speculation about the tomorrow of love."

"Would you really? Would you choose bright frocks in a meadow long ago or the ulti-mate romance of romance? I wonder."

"Bright frocks in a meadow long ago are a proper subject for art. Ultimate romance of romance is no proper subject for art. It's the difference between a lyric poem and a tract."

"Pardon — not at all! It's the difference be-tween a lyric written today and a lyric to be written a hundred years from now."

"But that will be a hundred years from now — if I am clear."

"You would say that art may not treat of futurity."

"I know that it may not. The artist is a re-corder, that is all. He is a recorder of more than other people see — that alone is why he is cre-ative. He is a recorder of more than other peo-ple see in our common experience, and in that alone."

" The common experience of today. Not of tomorrow. . . ."

" Certainly not of tomorrow. Of today."

" Of whose today? "

Round the circle again, and he had it all to do over, painstakingly, beautifully: " The to-day of anybody who responds to a clear inter-pretation of emotion. Love faced with death holds more for art today than does love in some unpredictable seventh heaven."

" I am not convinced. For in 1902 I met Tesla. I had my first prediction of the wireless. That moment, I assure you, meant more to me than bright frocks in a meadow. . . ."

" Or love faced with death? "

" . . . No, but with a meaning akin to it. Akin to it far more than to any bright frock! Was that moment of mine not a subject for art? "

" Absolutely not."

" Yet Tesla himself — and his work-room and his clothes and his cat, these were art's materials."

" Undoubtedly."

" How can that help reminding me of a neighbor who knew every bird, by name, note, and flight, but was bored at being told the names of the constellations? "

" How can that help reminding me of the girl I was once making love to who suddenly said: ' How glorious the stars are tonight! '

That which we call art could deal with my love, but it couldn't bother with Arcturus."

"But you are saying that there is no room in art for anything but the evident — the evident of evident people!"

"I am saying that there is room for all the *frisson* you can extract from the evidence!"

"Just so long, you mean, as it is never said?"

"*Frisson?* Said?"

"Dreiser's story: you think that he should not have broken into his history of Ida Hauchawout by crying in his own person: ' Mesdames and Messieurs! What is it all about? . . .' "

"He should never have committed that crime. I remember it well. He should have omitted everything from there to the final master information about Widdel's not knowing how to slice corn-meal mush."

"Why? Why? *Why?*"

"Because art deals with the ascertainable."

The Celebrated Author had won. But she thought of the Stone Age. Would a Stone Age novelist, by hinting at the Golden Age, have ruined his book?

Of a day when if witches sank they were innocent, and if they swam they were guilty. If a witch novelist had written of witchless days to come, would he have missed divine fire?

Of the truth that life is short and art is long. Shall the material of art be limited by life, or even by the past plus the period of the artist?

Of timelessness. The past, imaginatively re-created, belongs to art — today, imaginatively interpreted, belongs to art. If one imaginatively conceives tomorrow, that also shall not art claim?

Furthermore, an imaginative conception of tomorrow may not be of tomorrow alone, but of today discerned — already ascertainable! — to the creative artist. What is reality but the divination of the amœba become the ascertainable by the mollusk? And shall the amœba of today deny to art his own divination of either the amœba of today or the mollusk of tomorrow?

Yet — lest he be taken at unfair advantage, the Celebrated Author shall have the last word, which may declare the whole matter:

" After all," he said, " does it not reduce itself to intention? "

CHAPTER VIII

The Novel and the Spirit

I

A FEW YEARS AGO it was the habit of the New
York newspapers to instruct their reporters
that, whatever the nature of the story which
they brought to the city room, one rule must
be regarded: the story must be reduced to the
briefest possible statement and this statement
would constitute the first paragraph of the
newspaper account.

Thus: Clarence Thorne, eight-year-old son
of Mr. and Mrs. C. E. Thorne, living at 500
West Five Hundredth Street, was run over by
a sprinkling cart yesterday afternoon at four
o'clock as he was playing before his parents'
door, and was instantly killed.

Recently I read in the New York *Times* an
account of a similar accident, and the account
ran like this:

The children living in West Five Hundredth
Street wish that yesterday had not been a holiday because, if it had not been so, little Clarence Thorne, eight-year-old son of Mr. and
Mrs. Clarence Thorne, living at No. 500,
would have been busy at school with his books
instead of playing at hopscotch in the street
before his parents' door, where yesterday afternoon at four o'clock he met his death.

This opening paragraph tells the story, to be sure, briefly, and yet in so different a tone from its first statement that the paragraph may be said to regard a new ruling. Very few years have crept between the two fashions, but the whole feeling of the treatment has changed.

Certain habits of the novel vary quite as nimbly. As in *Père Goriot*, when the misfortunes of the Pension Vauquer have gathered and multiplied, one guest after another has dropped away, even that admirable Vautrin, of whom they made a convict; and to Madame Vauquer, receiving blow after blow, the final one is administered by Sylvie, the maid, who enters and cries out that the cat is missing: " Madame, I have not seen Mistigris for three days." " Ah, this . . ." cries Madame. The poor creature lifted her hands to her head. . . .

Imagine a modern novelist seeking to heighten a situation by a device like that. In such an hour he would be far more likely to introduce Sylvie saying that the green grocer had come for his order and would Madame have beans.

But however the mode of expression of a news story may vary, the character of the news itself remains unaltered. News is news. All the news is the news. News may be colored or suppressed, but to the city room and the public it is none the less news and has remained essentially the same since news-writing attained a professional status. It is only recently that the novel has attained to this honest estate. For though the novel has been slowly extending its technical frontiers, changing its style even as the newspaper, yet it is only of late that the novel has, so to say, begun to try to include all the news.

It is a great moment in any art when the artist transfers his attention from the extension of his method to the extension of his material. From a preoccupation with technical areas and rebellion at their limitations, the novelist seems now to have come to the unique delight of the artist; namely, such strong excitement in the presence of life that he must express that excitement. And if it is said that he has always been doing this, yes, he has done this for crises, for moments of extreme action, for acute situations, for the comedy, the tragedy, the zeniths, and the nadirs; but never before has he done this for life's sheer deadly death-dealing routine. As a gatherer of materials he now rivals the newspapers and is saying: " All the news for the novel, whether the public knows it as news or not." He is on his way from the old artificial selectiveness to a new selectiveness of still unknown standards.

Consider these three family-groups and their comparative value to the fiction-writers of today and yesterday:

The setting for the first is Portage, Wisconsin, where lives alone a woman in the eighties, alert, humorous, tolerant, well, who refuses to give up her home of a lifetime to go to live with children and grandchildren in the same town. " Here I stay," she says decisively; " I will go forth and back, but here I stay." And among all the many members of that family there is a relationship so tender that it would not be welcome material for any modern novelist. — Over the hill are three or four houses tenanted by members of a second family, and these continually at war. They do not admire one another's in-laws, and a pending property-distribution darkens the sky. Winds of bitterness and clamor rock those houses, and the town hears the impact. Rich material this, for any novelist of any period. — But now in the " residence part," as the townsfolk say, there is a third group, of whom the town has a stock observation: " Aren't the Blanks a lovely family? " In this family are the father, a business and church pillar of hackneyed composition; the mother, who does her best as a matter of course and never questions either; the three adult daughters, potentially charming women, without the initiative or the independence to accept life; and the one adult son, Gracchus — a model. " Gracchus Blank is such a nice man," says the town. In that home the thoughts of 1895 are household

words. A patriarchal family, with money.
And the town says: " Aren't the Blanks a
lovely family? "

Now of these three families the first, the
tender family, and the second, the bitter family, have often furnished legitimate news for
the novelist. So has the third, the patriarchal
family, as viewed by the townspeople. But the
novelist of today has discovered the breakfast-
table and the luncheon-table and the evening
lamp of that third family, not in crises, but
day by day. And he has discovered what goes
on within the pillar and the painstaking
mother and the three daughters and Gracchus,
the model, judged, not by the standards of the
town, but to some extent by the standards of
the new knowledge concerning renunciation
and repression and hypocrisy and business and
the Church. And the transvaluation of that
patriarchal family thus requires a new geometry, and all but requires another space. Not,
observe, that family in crises so much as that
family at breakfast, living its routine life much
as you and I live ours.

Of course the novelist has always handled
such a family if he could satirize it, blur it,
trick it, caricature it. But to record it has not
interested him. Indeed under the old theology,
the old sociology, the old psychology, he could
not record it because he did not see it. So he
was content to cover circumstance with some-

thing like the bright veil which we throw about the late doings of the dead.

Especially has he been content to use those bright veils in the ceremonies incident to his two most ancient incantations. Two valid incantations the novel has always known, the novel of every land which knows the novel: namely, romantic love, in an exhaustless number of colorful arrangements; and moral aspiration. On these virtually all novels have depended for their breath. Love and honor.

And among us these two enchantments have been pronounced in but one tongue and according to one tradition, the Anglo-Saxon. Not only has the American novel clung steadfastly to these two interests, but for years it never departed from the Anglo-Saxon interpretation of these two interests. Now of late the American novelist has made two discoveries.

The first discovery is that the American novel may treat of romantic love and moral aspiration not according to the Anglo-Saxon tradition, but according to the Anglo-Saxon habit of life — quite another matter.

The second discovery is that love and idealism are after all only two of the factors of existence; and that a large part of even the Anglo-Saxon life is occupied with neither the one nor the other.

Here are thus opened to the novelist masses

of fresh material in whose treatment, so far as
the Anglo-Saxon habit of life is concerned, it
is impossible for him to be imitative. It is the
opening up of a new country. His country, his
own people, as they are and not as they think
they are. His native sources of supply.

These native sources of supply are not
identical with 1776 and 1849 and 1865 and
1917. Nor, in spite of the sins of many, do they
depend upon the use of bad English. Gradually in New England, in Virginia, in Indiana,
in California, in New York, and, with Hamlin
Garland, and with Glenway Westcott's *The
Grandmothers,* in Wisconsin, mine after mine
of these native supplies has begun to yield its
peculiar ore, an ore not so much dependent
upon the dynamite of plot as upon a mere surface shovel to reveal its shining. For it is merely
the immemorial richness of human relationship as touched specifically by two influences.
One, and that one of lesser importance, is regional color. The second and inestimably the
more vital is the national genius. Regional color
has often been far too thickly overlaid, has become the " local discoloration " into which
Wilde saw local color degenerating. To the national genius the novel of any nation will always be delivered.

The distinctive fashion in which the desire
for growth and change expresses itself is the
manifestation of the genius of a nation. In the

American national genius we have a spirit now considerably crippled, but still recognizably at one with the spirit of the colonies and therefore now definitely at variance with many traditions, both native and world traditions, crystallized in unforeseen forms. For it seems that the right of the individual to life, liberty, and the pursuit of happiness is not limited, as we had earlier supposed, by his politics and his religion. And with this emphasis the national novel is now concerned, in common with the novels of the rest of the world. The novelist who is creative is bound to extend the principles of the national genius and is found applying it to all else which affects the growth of the individual: marriage, the great American home, relatives, institutions, conventions, traditions, and the accepted virtues in the routine of his civilization. But if crude aspects of this routine are presented by him, or crude characters questioning this routine at any point, somebody is going to say: " I don't like that book. It isn't about pleasant people. I shouldn't care to know them. Why write about them? " Conceivably it may not be about pleasant people. What are we going to do about it? Change the novel or change the people?

Recently in an evening of discussion on the English novel I heard a distinguished professor of science declare that all that he wanted of a novel was help in forgetting himself. That seems a crass confession, akin to one which might be made by a devotee of the motion picture. Developed drama or a symphony does not help one to forget oneself — it deepens one's sensibilities. It is this which one may ask of any art. It is this which one may ask of the novel. In that case the man of science was right, though not in the way that he meant. For to deepen one's sensibilities is of course to take one out of one's lesser self into one's wider incarnations.

It is precisely this process which, by a method known to the most elementary logic, the modern English novelists, including the American novelists, have more or less unconsciously begun to attempt. See, they say, not your greater incarnation, but its opposite, for so long not considered news for the novel at all. Read of the complacent deaths which you live; if you like, count them — if you can. And thus drop deeper into your pit, where you may better see the star of our potential life. Of course, as a matter of fact they say nothing of the sort. They merely let us enter the dark and they leave us there to dream of the light if we have it in us.

The following is quoted from an American novel:

The butcher had a hooked nose and when he smiled his nose seemed to press down his thick brown moustache that framed his even teeth so beautifully. He settled his apron over his stomach and gazed at her hungrily above the glass top of the counter as though he were trying to hypnotize her into buying some of the coral pink sausages which reposed beside a block of ice in the transparent case. . . . The meat shop was as white as death. It smelled of blood and sawdust. . . . " I want a — can you give me a nice rib roast today? What do you ask for those hens? " Mrs. Farley as always hesitated when she spoke. Her vague squinting eyes traveled undecidedly over the big pieces of meat, the shoulders, the forelegs, the haunches . . . the fowls dangling in a row a little before the meat. " I will take two of the hens," said Mrs. Farley. " Be sure you give me fat ones," she added frowning. She fumbled . . . for the money. She made her way through the bitter-smelling gloom.

And so on. Intolerable, certainly. But the novel did not manufacture the butcher-shop. It merely confessed it. Or this:

Dr. Beach had gone, but the nurse was still in the room. She had her back turned to the door and was folding up some clothes. The gas flame had been extinguished. The window curtains were open. Objects in the room were plainly visible, throwing no anchorage of shadow. Lawrence went toward the bed. He set his feet down carefully as if he were afraid of being heard. When he reached Her he saw She had not moved. She would never move. A sob of agony and relief shook him. . . . He knelt down by the bed. . . . She had not moved. . . . Stillness revolved about him in eternal motion.

Obviously *The Narrow House* did not manufacture that terrible sob of agony and relief. Or the terrible commonplace of the story which led up to it. Our novels have been accustomed for long to the good taste of hypocrisy. We have never been willing to admit life in art any more than in life.

However, there is now no hypocrisy, there are no veils, there is not even good taste in the novels intent on leading us into the dark and leaving us there to listen to its terrible breathing. All the news about living goes into these novels. And it is with this wholesale process that the use of the commonplace is concerned. In a majority of the realistic American novels of today we have a voice, not of evil, but of the commonplace. It is as if all the banalities of our lives — brushes, combs, coat-hangers, the defiling and scouring of dishes, the idiotic recreations, the stodgy generalizations, the sad commercialism, the tragic nothings which collect about us were suddenly to cry out in a single voice in these books. And you hear the naïve antiphonal chorus: " I don't like those books. . . . I shouldn't care to know the people." It is wholly unimportant whether or not we like the people. In some of our moments all of us are those people. Such novels are merely saying: " Look at us." And why should not the realistic novel say that which is being said by a laboring music, a fourth-dimensional art, and an ambiguous social order: " Look at us — us gods, fallen into more kinds of pit than seems possible "? These are no trumpet voices, no pulses of propaganda. They are mere recording voices, conversational, table-talking voices saying: " My dear gods, not only in your crises, but at your very breakfasts you are in a pit of your digging."

We have, then, in the American novel of to-day the facing of the Anglo-Saxon habit of life, the admission that it concerns itself with other things than love and aspiration, a tardy turning to our native sources of supply, the recognition of the value of the commonplace, and at last an honest expression of the national genius. But is there anything which the American novel signally lacks? What other material, in what way conditioned, might the novel require in its business of imaginatively recording us? Are there any sources of material which we here in America are neglecting? Is there any omission by which we are flawing our fiction as hypocrisy once flawed it? Has the American novel a malady?

The malady of our novels is an immemorial malady; namely, their lack of power to express beauty. Beauty as a force. Inhering beauty. Almost, one adds, incommunicable beauty.

II

" Beauty old, yet ever new, eternal voice and inward word." The momentary lift and urge which comes from the reading of that line carved on the New York Library façade, what novel can ever capture and sustain that? Perhaps it cannot yet be sustained in a novel, cannot even be borne by us, as it could not be borne to see a god. And yet it is a part of life, operative in beings. And there is that other line carved on the same façade, " But above all things truth beareth away the victory." Without beauty a record of truth is like the Borglum gargoyle at Princeton — the ill-equipped thing, having one arm and one wing. The novel which has not beauty has but one aspect of truth. And where in the American novel have we beauty?

We have it occurring here and there in volumes which will present themselves at once — well-remembered bits from Mrs. Wharton, from Howells, from James; from a half-dozen of the moderns. Something of beauty lurks in the work of many whom we moment by moment recall. But not enough beauty. Beauty has never yet been captured even approximately by any of them. Not captured, one may say, so nearly in the novel as Henry Adams captured it in the " Hall of Dynamos " — and there at the last it eluded him too. In the novel as America has developed it, there is offered as yet no veiled wonder.

As between that which we called beauty in the novel fifty years ago and phases of that which we call merely realism now, you and I may prefer the merely realistic, phases of which indeed may have become our idea of beauty. Beauty changes its form. Consider one worn instance of beauty, an instance to which we were long accustomed to refer as the loveliest chapter in the Victorian novel — the meeting of Richard Feverel and Lucy by the weir. We still love it, but do we not love it indulgently, as we love Cruikshank? Lift beside it a page of Conrad, a mere hurrying wing of a sail in the dark and brooding figures black against a red moon, intent in talk which is half eloquent elision — and we know that beauty, such as we have, has changed its form. Or in *The Rescue* the meeting of the two women, the catching up of the reality behind the racial difference, the reaching up to an evolutionary meaning, the dramatization of the cleft cut by centuries of breeding, the delicate shadowing forth of all that is to come, the fascination of the fragile yet firm effects won by every flawless sentence; and from restraint that always rhythmic slip back to the gorgeous tapestry of the tropics, all this sustained with other and yet other strands interwoven — the unconscious genius of love in Linyard, the genius of his friend of the one great passion; the whole forever pointing, pointing to the inevitable imperious — but how melodramatic! — conclusion: " Steer north! " This is beauty as we know it now in the novel; and incidentally it is of the essence of Cônrad. By it we mean infinitely more than the beauty of a mosaic. We mean the beauty of an organism.

But even organic beauty such as is fundamental to *The Rescue* is to be transcended. There is beauty already actually incarnate in life, but in novels seldom operative and never treated as casually existent, like flowers. For refinements of human conduct have run far ahead of their reflection in the novel — the novel is still intent on crude aspects of behavior already by at least a measurable proportion of the race left behind.

Certainly, the use of the Ten Commandments as direct fictional motives has been outgrown. Characters in fiction who ordered their lives under the conscious stimulus of the Ten Commandments would be ridiculous. The Ten Commandments as immediate dictators of action obviously have no literary value. It is only in that area which lies beyond precept, in the shadowy caves of cross-current and countercurrent that the novel can employ them at all.

But among these derivatives the novel seems usually to seize upon crass examples. Witness that highest moment in *The Rescue* — Linyard's resolute " Steer north! " The moment when the yacht has left the island and has taken away all that Linyard cared for in the world:

. . . Carter approached him and spoke quietly.

" The tide has turned and the night is coming on. Hadn't we better get away from these shoals, sir? " . . .

Linyard came out of his absorption with a deep tremor of his powerful frame like the shudder of an uprooted tree.

" How was the yacht heading when you lost sight of her? " he asked.

" South, as near as possible," answered Carter. " Will you give me a course to steer for the night, sir? "

Linyard's lips trembled before he spoke, but his voice was calm. " Steer north," he said.

Here is one of the exalted moral beauties of the novel — renunciation. And yet in *The Rescue* — and how much more patently in the novels of any other — what a grandiose gesture it is! " Steer north " is clear melodrama. Renunciation represents a stage in human conduct, but it may be a crude stage. We have James and Conrad as apostles of renunciation and on their heels comes a psychology isolating and defining repression, so that already there dawns for us the gospel of transmutation: not to deny or to renounce, but to transcend; not to waste force, but to transform it; not to thwart, but to exceed; to turn passion into power. Here are fields for the fortitude and the delicacy of the novelist beside which undiscriminating renunciation is as crude as blind obedience. Here fall nuances of creative conduct beside which " Steer north " bears an odor of bad taste, insisting too much — as does

the Golden Rule, that precept for the child in
process of becoming so sensitized that he will
do unto others the right for its own sake.
But these and their like are favorite nobili-
ties of the novel — the glorified detective-
story with a man himself as both culprit and
keeper; or of late as pleased fugitive from the
whole case.

Now, there are in the world countless per-
sons of humor and variety for whom certain
moral struggles no longer exist. There are those
in whose conduct money questionably
touched could enter no more than murder;
by whom the truth is spoken quite as simply
and naturally as good English; in whom good
faith is not an accomplishment, like harp-
playing, but a function, like sight; those in
whom the social consciousness is a passion beside which any personal profit can live not
even as an impulse; those who do not brawl in
their families or shout "me first," in any of
its tongues. Those whose reactions are in the
main socialized, spiritualized, humanized. And
who — the point is here — are conscious of
but a quite ordinary functioning. No grandiose gestures from them! Merely records of
reaction, rich in humor and misadventure and
delight and deep waters: the old, dreaming beyond dreams; youth, with its new æsthetic;
the middle generation, understanding neither;
folk of pressing preoccupations, inarticulacies,

flashes of insight; of heart-breaking misapprehension, memories, inevitabilities; who go rekindling old fires; what have these tragedies to do with raw " right " and " wrong "? Great areas of living involve for such folk as these no crude moral choices at all. But they are rarely admitted to the pages of the modern novel, at least without a fanfare. Their moral matter-of-course becomes in the novel heavily featured. Good faith and the social passion, for example, are there employed in isolated self-conscious moments, not called casual but made crucial; or else are challenged, revalued, abandoned.

Eventually we shall have, we must believe, occasional novels taking for granted a certain degree of moral health and going about a brighter business. Indeed this may be the only way in which we shall succeed in getting rid of self-conscious idealism as a root motif of the novel, an idealism to which the Anglo-Saxon novel-reader clings as tenderly as the Anglo-Saxon in his daily life likes to believe that he himself clings. We shall be rid of this motif not by challenging order or by stopping in the welter on this side, but by writing of those who have transcended chaos.

" Do you not see," offers the devotee of the " red-blooded " novel, " with the use of such material you'd have no novel? Because you'd have no struggle."

But we hear the unimaginative say that if the economic struggle were removed, life would not be worth living. The novel in which a crude moral struggle, either lost or won, is the highest motif is as primitive in art as is the economic struggle in life.

Also the reader of the red-blooded novel holds that such serene folk are too rare to become suitable fiction material. Even if they are rare, they should have in the novel a place as secure as the pathologic and the drunken, who seem always to be welcome. The sophisticated reader ventures that by such novels we should be dangerously approaching, in the usual spiral of experience, an apotheosis of the condition through which the novel earlier took its way: the perfect family relationship, the perfect love, perfection *ad nauseam*. Even if this were true, it would not matter. The novel must deliver itself to material which bears no relation to self-conscious perfection. It is precisely the weakness of Anglo-Saxon morality and novel-making alike that they can imagine no such material.

Yet in experience it is not until " temptations " are left behind that really beautiful living can begin. Previous to that time everything is crude and experimental. All the loveliest nuances of relationship lie in the region beyond such voices. Human experiences reveal new faces in this clear air. Whole planes of experience are to be treated for which only the reasonably evolved can possibly furnish material. And always there is the free spirit within in fleeting union with an exquisite and inexorable spirit without — the great inner history, useless, or no more than incidental to the novel so long as the shackles of a crude idealism have not fallen away. Nor need these adventures by any means be confined to the sophisticated, the formally choice. Homely hearts and hearths furnish their high proportion of unconscious fineness — the unconscious, which always matters most. Theirs are the choices to some extent already bred into the race.

The chief concern of the American novel of tomorrow will be to uncover the beauty of our essential commonplace living as the novel of today has triumphantly uncovered its ugliness. To uncover beauty not by denying ugliness — the novel of today has made that forever impossible — but first by accepting all of life, something which we in America have never been willing to do either in art or in life; and then by a new selectiveness. It is only after a broadly affirmative art arises that a really selective art becomes possible. The modern realistic novel performs the inestimable service of extending our admissions, our affirmations. It has chosen to affirm the commonplace, the sordid, the ugly, because that is most obvious;

also it is far easier to record; is, in fine, the natural gesture away from sentimentality and hypocrisy and smugness. Of course the gesture has been too violent. As Conrad says in his *Notes on Life and Letters*:

> It seems as if the discovery made by many men at various times that there is much evil in the world were a source of unholy joy unto some of the modern writers. It gives an author — goodness only knows why — an elated sense of his own superiority. And there is nothing more dangerous than such an elation to that absolute loyalty towards his feelings and sensations an author should keep hold of in his most exalted moments of creation.

And it is true that the novel here in America, having at last eaten of the tree of good and evil and of the commonplace — doubtless unknown in Eden — has learned to admit not only that life is not all apples, but has occasionally led us to suppose that orchards bear exclusively cores — or even worms.

There is, however, nothing ultimately pessimistic about our present records of the commonplace. Nothing inexorable is expected by these modern novels to crush us. There is in them no sense of fate — that is not the way of the national genius. Even Mr. Hergesheimer in his records of a debased society, though he is ironic, is still rather wistful. All these novels are merely saying: " Look at us, gods in the pit — but a pit of our own digging. And we are worth digging out. If we were not so, we shouldn't have mentioned it."

This so far is the sum of their affirmations; a broad enough extension if one considers the inhibitions of the nineties, when our novels were either formed for vigilance committees or else were " light."

So in the revealing of life to which every generation of novelists succeeds, their entire work has as yet hardly touched at life's inner magic. And the greatest of this magic, it is predictable, will be the magic of love. It may be against love that the sins of our modern novels are greatest. For it may appear that love is only one aspect of that heightening of faculty and perception towards which the race seems to be tending. Or what if it is true that the extensions of faculty of the race are to be developed by those in the heightened perception known as " being in love? " Consider what may lie in store for us when novels shall reflect these courts. Picture that sort of love-story and compare it with our love-stories of now, with the hackneyed lure of the Third-at-the-threshold, the use of the pathologic, the drunken. To these the novel is still serving its brief bondage.

Poetry, pictorial and plastic art, and music, all so much more highly developed than fiction or than the society which fiction now depicts, have always risen to that medium of expression which now we seek for the novel — expression which does not merely record beauty, but rises to the actual planes of beauty itself.

It is upon these lovely areas that fiction must adventure. It must know beauty, it must be beauty. Not the beauty of the flesh, but the beauty of the cell and of its unknown urge. Inhering beauty. The beauty of our essential living.

CHAPTER IX
The Novel of Tomorrow

I

ALREADY WE HAVE MOSAICS of beauty in the American novel. But it lacks organic beauty.

In the modern novels of England the high example of organic beauty seems to be the work of Hudson. No one knows what he does; but his touch unseals an essence.

In the American novel we have nothing approaching this essence. One is grateful, in these days of the triumphant discovery of the commonplace, for mere beautiful mosaics. But these have little to do with the basic beauty, the organic beauty which a novel must breathe before it can approximate its potential scope and function.

Organic beauty in any art usually consists of beauty not already familiar to us. Familiar beauty can give us the mosaics. But it is strangeness in beauty which alone can weave the spell and bear the perfume. This is not to say unreality; but on the contrary a deeper reality than we are accustomed to divine. The reality of literal levels of perception to which we do not ordinarily penetrate or of which, rather, we are not often conscious as they penetrate our own plane. Professor Eucken's claim that the spiritual world is " an independent reality, waiting to be apprehended, waiting to be incorporated into our universe " is enormously served by art, whose functioning is so largely in extensions of the ordinary faculties. Between the naturalistic novel, which is a record, and the romantic novel, which is the product of human imagining, lies this other novel, the novel of tomorrow, concerned with imminent yet almost undivined reality of human conduct, human dream, perceived " for their own sakes, with the eyes of disinterested love."

Our failure may lie in the fact that such beauty as our novels have is chiefly concerned with moral idealism and romantic love, as we know them now. Our moral idealism is still intent on the esoteric with — shall we say? — either simple standards which ought long ago to have been taken for granted or conventionalized standards having no correspondence with the mystery of conduct. Therefore our novels devote themselves, for example, to one emerging from a crude upbringing to the point of being hounded by her " furies " to escape tawdriness. Or even with those records of Henry James, that, Conrad calls him — that " historian of the individual conscience, of adventure in which only choice souls are involved " — crucial instances, always suffused with a certain beauty. And as for the treatment in novels of romantic love, that is always a matter of bright feathers, of the *pas seul*, our only advance from that cave-door courting being that there are antiphonal feathers and dancing. In spite of the fact that there is, both in idealism and in love, something not ourselves which is the glory of the experience, still the novel continues to treat only of measurable reactions, rarely calling down the utter sunlit areas where every human soul does some time enter. Now these sunlit areas are a part of life, of reality. If they can be experienced, they can be incarnated in the novel. And it is these sunlit spaces of discernible reality which can give to the novel a new basis of beauty.

Such reaches are not merely extensions of moral idealism or of romantic love. Neither the one nor the other may be of dominating concern there, save in some form so heightened that it has passed into pure beauty. These areas are not remote; it is their power that they interpenetrate the homeliest lives and the most ordinary surroundings. This is a point which the worshipper of mosaics of beauty will not readily admit, and perhaps about his mosaics he is right. But organic beauty is everywhere at home.

The function of the novel is not to treat of life as it appears to the ordinary eye; or even to treat life in its ordinary aspect, if that were ascertainable. It is not even to treat of life as it should be, if *that* were ascertainable. Its function is not primarily to report the familiar at all. The function of the novel is to reflect the familiar as permeated by the unfamiliar; to reflect the unknown in its daily office of permeating the known.

Thus the novelist is to go not only " joying in his visible universe," but in that universe by which his own is interpenetrated. That universe invisible save as music or color or the word or some other high manifestation causes it to flower in human experience.

It is this high manifestation of the word which Hudson makes. He causes unfamiliar verities to enter our ken as verities. For the poetic mind, the mind, then, of the novelist at his best, is the perceiver of the real curve of life, the knower of something at least of its inner ecstasy.

II

. . . How shall this interpretation best be made? This accomplishment concerns the form of the novel. However extreme has been the modern novel in stressing the commonplace, it has accomplished a form suitable for the expression of reality. Any reality, commonplace or not. This form is direct, unreflective, highly selective. It is in immediate contact with its material. It is uncompromising, tactless, unashamed. And its style is as bare and clear as a plain.

It may be that the whole flair for the commonplace will be found to have contributed chiefly to the formation of a new purity of form. The treatment of the commonplace calls for stark precision, and, by treating the commonplace, the novel has learned something of stark precision. If the novel had continued to treat of "the good, the true, and the beautiful," it might be laboring on, with the redundance of that phrase itself, in a fringed and silken fashion, tasseled, plumed, melancholy.

When the novel can take that form — that naked and lovely instrument — and that stark style, and cause them to function in the expression of nameless beauty, such as Hudson summons, it will have sounded the new note, the note of the novel of tomorrow. And this will be a note of romanticism, but not of romanticism as we have ever known it.

Ten years ago a wise man said: "Free verse is all well enough. It is now a vehicle for many who otherwise would have no vehicle. But wait until the poets begin to use it. *Then!*"

So it is of the terse, the staccato, the compact, the shorn form and style of the modern American novel. Heighten its compactness, take from it certain affectations, such as deliberate sordidness, saturate it with all that divination can capture of communicable beauty. " *Then!* "

To use his divination to clarify the inter-penetrating beauty of common life and to draw down still other beauty; not to manu-facture it from unreality, but to discern it in reality and to reflect it; and then to pour this beauty through the clear crystal of a form as honest as a milk-bottle — there lies the novel-ist's lovely, his imperative task.

But this he will never do if he is working with his mind alone. Only when he knows that his divination of beauty, of all life, is " an independent growth which he himself tends and watches," will be incarnate in the novel the vast and lovely proportion of the days.

CHAPTER X
Beauty and the Commonplace

IT BECOMES EVER MORE EVIDENT that there is a mode of beauty existing on another plane and that it is the province of art to draw into our own plane this beauty. It is also the province of other agencies. For example, of spring, of love, of religion.

No one fails to understand that this is true of love: the color of rose is over the world for lovers. The lure of elsewhere is in the air of spring. And there is the unearthly happiness of the saint. At one with all these is the nascent joy of the artist in creation. He is a channel for the birth of beauty into our medium. He becomes so by some special grace of seeing; by that which is the beginning of all wisdom; by a heightening of perception akin to the experience which the East knows as illumination; a breaking through to another level of being to which the race shall in time come as to its own inheritance. Meanwhile the artist is the reporter of that other plane.

As to the characteristics of this domain of beauty, these reporters seem to be generally agreed. First of all, it bears an air of Elsewhere. Most painters, good or bad, have somehow caught some vestige of this hidden and lovely air — you may fathom it in their landscapes, occasionally in the eyes of their portraits, more rarely in their passionate searching to speak out in color. There these things are, somewhere in the " rolled-back air," for the artist to see, and he spends his life in trying to tell his fellows that there is literally Somewhere else to be.

Recently in the corridor of a beautiful hotel I was faced by some admirable gray wall-paper, a reproduction of an earlier period. A pleasaunce, a fountain, chestnuts, distance. But there it was! The designer had seen and he had known. And abruptly there stood out the triumphant and accusing argument uttered by the spendthrifts of the world, the spendthrifts of taste and imagination. For they also, creators of pleasaunce and court splendor, wasters of the people, have sometimes glimpsed that vivid realm and have commanded men to create on this earth that paradise. To all lengths they have gone, exploiting their fellows, trampling, oppressing, violating every rule of that realm afar; all that they might decree pleasure-domes faintly to reflect that sovereign glory. A dignity for Kubla Khan! If a man or a nation is going to oppress anybody, he would far better do so for beauty than for black and yellow and brown men to fill his conscript armies.

A May morning; an orchard in bloom; a deep forest; dawn in a valley; the world from a mountain-top — all are momentary glimpses of some exquisite norm which overlies us, or interpenetrates us, waiting for us to catch its rhythm. And of all the men the artist is in some way equipped to catch that rhythm, to reflect that color, to divine that line, word, mass — as the saint reflects it in conduct, as the prophet reflects it in vision, as the child reflects it in his nature, as the entire race reflects it in dreams or in desultory moments of goodwill. But the artist is a channel from the very sources of beauty's renascence in us. He is one of the few remaining channels of religion, of relationship with spirit. He is beauty's supreme lover and interpreter.

What, then, has the artist to do with the recent harvest of realistic novels? What has he, as novelist, to do with photographic studies of American towns, and families, and their terrible commonplace?

Criticism has concluded that these are merely his cries in celebration of his escape from a cradle; a cradle over which sentimental talk and Anglo-Saxon precepts held the air, with wise and tender women in the house, and the poor and fallen wandering without; and with men either evil or — as indeed in novels the British public still insists — all lionlike and great. From his cradle the novelist saw that the evil may be also the good, and for a time he played with the toy of that discernment. Next he saw that the " good " may be the evil, a harder matter to divine; and he is still taking a devilish and holy and useful delight in such divination. After these leisurely preparations he escaped his cradle, rose, and regarded his family and the neighbors. Then he understood how many of these lack the force to be either good or evil and how in their terrible commonplace they confuse the two, confuse everything and everybody and insist that all is for the best. It is not wonderful that at this experience the novelist has gone out of his head and can think of nothing save imprecation. At a time when nationalism has imposed upon us the vastest complacence and cant of the ages, the least that the novelist can do, it has seemed to him, is to sit hard on the other end of the board. Such is the present occupation of him who is beauty's supreme lover and interpreter. And if we look no further we may well lose faith in him.

We have done even worse than lose faith in him. Instead of reproaching the novelist for seeing only complacence and cant and confusion, and instead of reproaching the human family for so industriously manifesting these, we have been tirelessly reiterating: " I don't like such people. I shouldn't care to know them. They depress me." Tenable as a criticism of life — if one is that sort. Not even

relevant, one would say at first, as a criticism
of art.

But is the fault with the novelist for con-
fessing too much of the commonplace; or with
us for manifesting no more of beauty for him
to divine; and is the criticism, after all, deeply
relevant, far more so than the critic knows?

The fault is both with the novelist and with
us, but his fault is the greater since he it is who
has a special grace of seeing, who has that
" awareness which is the beginning of wisdom " ; and since it is the artist who is
beauty's supreme lover and interpreter. May
it not be that this discontent of criticism,
even in its maddening reiteration, bears a deep
relevance to art itself. For the novelist sees,
but does not express — and we know, but do
not manifest — and this the critic vaguely
feels, and wails: that there is a mode of beauty
existing on another plane and that it is the
province of art to draw into our own plane
this beauty.

Even the commonplace manifests on another plane, whose presence the artist, and
eventually we, must discern. Everybody does
discern it in faint flashings. But unless the
novelist looks alive he is going to express
merely the grotesquerie of the effort to seek it,
or the humor of the vainglory of having momentarily swayed to it, or the pathos of having missed it. He knows, however, that it is

there. And it is his task to isolate it, and then to reveal that inner norm to our own ragged and piping plane.

The fiction of the future will realize angels in the commonplace. It will clarify the beauty of much that we are accustomed to pass by.

You see in a Portage, Wisconsin, grocery a little anæmic man with enormous eyes buying for someone ten cents' worth of candy in a striped paper bag and giving painstaking care to the selection. This is not as dun as it seems, nor is it to be sentimentalized. It bears a certain beauty which you may catch and isolate and integrate. Not by merely looking at it. You do not catch the beauty of a loved face by merely looking at it, nor can you thus see any inner beauty. It must be evoked, rendered. This is not merely a process. It is a power.

There enters an elevator a stodgy and solid-colored pair, breathing visibly, laboring to persist. Somebody titters, and the woman's look flies out in intolerable anxiety. (Have they after all failed? Is somebody laughing at them?) There is to be evoked, rendered, almost a maternal feeling for these two, a terror at the babyishness of the adult heart, awe at its infantile idealism. The two in their flesh stand there like the mass of clay round which some dreaming sculptor has drawn gray cloths.

You hear a middle-aged woman playing at the piano an air which she has practiced to surprise her family. You hear her husband ask her if she would mind not playing. And you see her bright look as, misunderstanding him, she asks: " Did you say: ' Play it again ' ? " A dainty tragedy. And beauty. It is not only vast failures to co-ordinate which hold beauty and the tragic.

In all the deadliness of our routine there are colors — the reflected colors of that other plane. Pictorial art long ago discovered this mysterious beauty of the commonplace. The novelist has ceased to sentimentalize it, but he has slipped now to the other extreme of crying out only its manifest horror.

Manifestly, this defect of the modern novel is at one with our own inability to transmute our routine to the tenderer substance of the spirit; to let in upon life the airs of another level; to understand that life, like art, expresses itself primarily through a medium not technically its own. But if we do not know ourselves to have this power of surpassing ourselves, it is the business of the novelist to report on this common power so long unexercised — to record the beauty which we do not see, but which he does see, if he does.

Thus there is a valid right gropingly expressed by those who feel outraged at the commonplace and the sordid in the modern novel;

and who discern that there is a mode of beauty existing on another plane and that it is the province of art to draw it into our own. As it is the province of spring, of love, and of religion.

Now spring does not come often; love may fan light wings; the birdlike joy of religious exaltation is a hard-won home. But by a touch the artist, the novelist, can become the channel from all these sources, and from some inner corresponding area, for the birth of beauty into our medium. No wonder that when he fails to do this, we feel a grievance. *For we are ready.*

Or are we ready? When we try to tell him what we want him to do, all that we are able to say to him is: " Can't we have a little more sweetness and light? " — as if he were the porter and the car were stuffy. On which he rages and tells us that the way for us to have these things is for us to make them; that he cannot record what we do not manifest, and so on. Our answer is simple: Not every bit of us is incarnate, and it is his business to see us both in flesh and in spirit all the time. What else is a novelist for?

When such beauty does begin to be drawn through into the novel, as it has long been drawn in music, one wonders whether we shall indeed recognize it. Doubtless there will be those who will fall upon it and call it a mere romantic revival; and yet in the end it may be to these malcontents that we shall look for guidance. For such dissatisfaction when it is born of somebody very little lower than the angels takes a trail to heaven. Already the naturalistic novelist finds himself divinely dissatisfied. You catch a far look in his eye as now while he works and plays he grows conscious, it may be, of something else: a haze, a passing, a far light. He is reminded. He exclaims: "Oh, yes, beauty!" Then he "employs" beauty — a decoration, a relief, an exaltation, a point. But beauty as a bourne he has not yet entered. He has no right to wait for us to enter. The artist is beauty's supreme lover and interpreter.

CHAPTER XI
Scholarship and the Spirit

AT INTERVALS A NEW WORD, long known to everyone else, emerges for one and sounds above other words. For me such a word is "allotrope." That whose constituents, identical with those of something else, yet have a different molecular arrangement, so that the two present quite different aspects. We know that the diamond is loosely spoken of as the allotrope of coal — both carbon, but one a child of earth and the other kindred to the sun. We know that oxygen and ozone are allotropic. It is Mr. J. W. Thomson, in his English laboratory, who has lately announced that there exists an allotrope of water.

Now it may be that this allotrope of water will prove to be a substance denser than water, and a baser thing, as coal is denser than a diamond. The lay account of this which was given to me did not specify. But I like to think that the new substance will be more delicate, more exquisite, harder to imagine. Something as much finer and lovelier than water as a diamond is lovelier than coal. Imagine such a substance. How bright, how transparent, how shining. What undivined properties might it not have — what colors, what powers, what fragrances. It may be acted on by emanations and so open a whole corridor of new experience in perception. "And think," I heard a man say reverently, "think what it will do to us when we drink it." Perhaps the new race will some day be relating how we ancients brewed a strong and fiery and deathful fluid, from which we had to be restrained by law, when all the time there was awaiting us this possibility of entering upon new areas of most delicate experience by tasting the allotrope of water. As we creep about in this primordial ooze, with our faint toys of radium and radio and aeroplane, we can begin to dream what they will be perceiving and feeling when finer and fairer allotropes of other things have been discovered: of air, of fire, of earth, of ourselves. And we can beat the materialists on their own ground, for in order to enter into all such wonder it will not be necessary to change human nature, which they are so sure cannot be done. It will be necessary only to arrange our molecules a little differently — or it may be a good deal differently. Orville Wright and Langley did not change human nature when they put it in a plane. The figurative application is beyond words engaging, and brings us inevitably to the allotropes of art.

Loosely used to flash a meaning, without being more particular than is the lightning at its business of revealing both earth and heaven, the Elgin marbles and the scratching of the Aztecs are allotropic; the work of Greek sculptors and the images of the Egyptian gods are allotropic. And an allotrope of — shall we say? — *Clarissa Harlowe* is *Ethan Frome*. Of what divinable use are some physical facts save to permit us to make figures of them? . . .

When the stranger enters Ethan Frome's bare kitchen, and you understand that the withered, bright-eyed, piping cripple woman sitting there by the cold hearth with Ethan Frome's old wife is Mattie Silver, the vivid girl with whom you have watched him share the hour when they tried to die together, you have in a glare the black bulk of the years in which these three beings have lived together under one roof: Mattie, made lame and helpless by that catastrophe which was to have dealt death to her and to Ethan — Ethan's wife taking her in — Mr. and Mrs. Ethan Frome hostess to Mattie down the thirty years in which she grows ugly and querulous . . . without a comment, the horror of those years is hurled before you in a page, and by them you are shaken as by experience.

There is no need to go back to *Clarissa Harlowe*. Go back merely to *Jane Eyre*. To that night of horror when Jane, on the eve of her marriage to Mr. Rochester, wakes to see in her room his crazed wife trying on the wedding veil. Between the birth of that terrible visage

in the mirror, with the crude affirmation that
" the maniac bellowed," which used to keep
one awake nights, and the writing of that
single line, " This is Miss Mattie Silver," there
has been a rearrangement of the molecules of
the novel, resulting in hardly less than the discovery of a new substance. We have the same
ingredients, the same emotions, the same rela-
tions — but the one result is density, and the
other is a diamond.

Consider the types of men and women who
are appearing in our novels, not as " comic re-
liefs " or in any form of secondary rôle, but
as primary characters, as, if you like, " hero
and heroine." For example, Adrienne Toner, in
the important novel of that name by Anne
Douglas Sedgwick. But before we look upon
Adrienne, shall we look back upon an earlier
" heroine," upon Lucy in the moment of her
meeting with Richard Feverel in the celebrated
chapter called " Ferdinand and Miranda ":

She was indeed sweetly, fair, and would have been held
fair among rival damsels. . . . The wide summer-hat,
nodding over her forehead to her brows, seemed to flow
with the flowing heavy curls, and those fire-threaded
mellow-curls, only half-curls, waves of hair call them,
rippling at the ends, went like a sunny red-veined tor-
rent down her back almost to her waist: a glorious vision
to the youth, who embraced it as a flower of beauty, and
read not a feature. There were curious features of color
in her face for him to have read. Her brows, thick and
brownish against a soft skin showing the action of the

blood, met in the bend of a bow, extending to the temples
long and level: you saw that she was fashioned to peruse
the sights of earth, and by the pliability of her brows
that the wonderful creature used her faculty, and was
not going to be a statue to the gazer. Under the dark
thick brows an arch of lashes shot out, giving a wealth
of darkness to the full frank blue eyes, a mystery of
meaning — more than brain was ever meant to fathom:
richer, henceforth, than all mortal wisdom to Prince
Ferdinand. For when nature turns artist, and produces
contrasts of color on a fair face, where is the Sage, or
what the Oracle, shall match the depth of its lightest
look?

Here is the introduction to the character of
Adrienne Toner — a book of Anne Douglas
Sedgwick's, published in 1922:

> Miss Toner's was an insignificant little head, if indeed
> it could be called little, since it was too large for her
> body, and her way of dressing her hair in wide braids,
> pinned round it and projecting over the ears, added to
> the top-heavy effect. The hair was her only indubitable
> beauty. . . . It was cut in a light fringe across a pro-
> jecting forehead and her mouth and chin projected, too;
> so that, as he termed it to himself, it was a squashed-in
> face, ugly in structure, the small nose, from its depressed
> bridge, jutting forward in profile, the lips, in profile,
> flat yet prominent. Nevertheless he owned, studying her
> over his tea-cup, that the features, ugly, even trivial in
> detail, had in their assemblage something of unexpected
> force.

And then, if one is looking for a heroine,
what bewilderment to follow! Adrienne is the
cultivated Dulcy. She is the apotheosis of
Dulcy. She utters spiritualized bromides. She

doesn't say: " I never read a story serially. I always wait for it to come out in book form." But she says: " I'd rather say my prayers out of doors in the sunlight on a day like this, than in any church. I feel nearer God alone in His great world than in any church built with human hands. But we must all follow our own light." She doesn't say: " I've just washed my hair and can't do a thing with it." She says: " With all its excesses and ardors I have always felt the French Revolution to be a sublime expression of the human spirit." Infinitely removed from the Dulcy of the bus-top, she is the well-bred Dulcy of the best people, uttering the inanities of her kind. She speaks always of a " fine deep-hearted woman," of a " gifted girl," of a " rare sweet being." In moments of crisis her way of dealing is to quote with sweetness and light in her voice: " Heartily know, when half-gods go. . . ." She meets Roger Oldmeadow for the first time at a house-party and sees him cynical and bored. So after breakfast, as she is leaving, she engages him for a moment by the fireplace in the dining-room, and says: " Mr. Oldmeadow, you must trust more. Just try and trust."

Religious, patriotic, and spiritual cant make up her talk. She sings the terrible Me-first of a young civilization. My ideas first, my religion first, better than anybody's else ideas or religion or country. The cultured, internation-

ally minded, mellowed folk of an older civilization, with whose exponents she comes in
contact, find her far more subtly amusing than
that earlier American in Europe, Daisy Miller.
In fact, Adrienne Toner is to a later day, a day
which measures its subjects by psychological
tests, what Daisy Miller was to that Rome
which judged alone by standards of society and
its etiquette. Adrienne is the exponent of the
unrecognized Absurd in the talk of the informed, the well-bred. She is to the sensitized
what Dulcy is to the sophisticated. She is of
those called "finished" who utter themselves forth day after day in hand-me-down
thoughts. If you see no humor in the seminary
graduating class whose motto was: "Our boat
is launched, but where's the shore?" you will
see no humor in Adrienne. If you see no un-
bearable pathos in that motto, or in Dulcy,
neither in Adrienne will you see it.

And when life seizes her, shakes her, leaves
her desolate, and you have a new Adrienne, re-
organized, kindled to realities, illumined, then
not at all does she cease her platitudes. Here is
the perfection of Miss Sedgwick's art, that on
page 341 Adrienne talks just as she did in those
first revelations. Now she says to Oldmeadow,
by this time deeply in love with her and whom
she is refusing to marry:

" . . . the war, that has torn us all. But when it's
over, when you can go home again and take up your own

big life-work, happiness will come back. I'm sure of it.
We are all unhappy sometimes, aren't we? We must be;
with our minds and hearts. Our troubled minds, our
lonely hearts. . . ."

The drawing of the character is a beautiful
performance, a promise of discernment in the
fiction of tomorrow which has rarely been so
exemplified in the fiction of today. One is reminded of the characters in Disraeli's novels
(" Rise quickly, my love. Someone is approaching. It is a tramper! ") — only Disraeli's characters were taken for granted in a
mist, and Adrienne is under a microscope. A
microscope which reveals molecules in arrangements which the novels of yesterday never
even guessed at.

Richard Feverel and Adrienne Toner —
two novels, each compact of all that novels are
usually constituted of, human emotion, human
relationship, human charcteristic and choice
and their outcomes — and yet so different in
discovery and arrangement that they are virtually two distinct forms of art. Between Lucy
and Adrienne is the difference between the
worlds of Ptolemy and Copernicus. Lucy is
two-dimensional, a flat surface of type. Adrienne is round and revolving and intent upon
her individual orbit.

After Effie in *The Heart of Midlothian*, or
after Hester Prynne, there is the same discovery
and rearrangement to make before we come to

Sheila Kaye-Smith's magnificent Joanna Godden. Joanna is the study of a woman whose dominating masculinity of temperament hides a nature exquisitely feminine, a combination which, as one of the reviewers notes, always " proves irresistibly fascinating to a certain type of highly organized and spiritualized man." This type of woman is perfectly well known, but she has seldom been used as a primary character in fiction save in such figures as Katherine, the shrew to be tamed, who is tamed, as a matter of course; or as some wild heart which inevitably came to grief if it didn't get tamed; or for episode, as O. Henry presented such women. But Sheila Kaye-Smith gives you Joanna, big, touseled, capable, self-centered, alive, so that you love her as much as you do Portia or Rosalind. And when, on market day, this great Joanna strides through the crowd to the son of a neighbor baronet and says: " You and I should ought to be better acquainted," the reader does not look at her with the eyes of the baronet's son, not with the eyes of the tittering villagers, not with the eye of detachment, but the reader not less than approaches the man with Joanna. And thereafter walks with her throughout the book. Yet judged by every known standard of the old fiction, save for what was once called a character part, Joanna is impossible.

As material in fiction is thus differently

arranged, so style has necessarily followed after. Even with the humanity and poignancy of George Eliot, her long dissertations, her constant intrusions of authorship, are no longer tolerable. Even with the story-telling power of Scott we know now that when we used to skip his " fine writing," his " descriptive passages," we were fundamentally right, and that our sense of guilt was our literary taste, budding.

What is the significance of a new style, of these new choices of character? It is not that the author's skill tricks one into sentimental sympathy for Adrienne or Joanna. It is not only the infectious magic of the novelist's power of actual self-identification with " every kind of human life." It is not only that power transferred to the reader to identify himself with " the failure, the futility, the finiteness of all human beings "; with that which Dreiser calls their " somehow pitiable finiteness in the midst of infinity." It is not only because of our new enthusiasm for honesty, for disillusion, even for ugliness. No, it is more than these: it is the novelist's, the artist's, the creator's discovery that the old arrangements of human values actually have somehow been superseded, and that behind the ordinary aspect of quite ordinary things and ordinary folk, in ordinary reactions, there is visible a new pattern of the old spiritual treasure.

At intervals, in any art, this new arrangement takes place. The gnarled and knotted face in the monotype of a Provincetown art student today differs from portraiture of two decades ago not primarily in method, but in that the artist of the monotype has made an arrangement of Man never before ventured upon, and has thus discerned an aspect of Man never before quite detected. We may not like the new reality or we may, but the point is that by this rearrangement of old materials, we have broken through to see more Man, more Woman, more Animal, more Thing — more Life. It was always there, but we have rearranged it, have caused it to leap out at us in a new guise — like a diamond in the coal-bin. These new valuations of the familiar come to everyone in daily living. Edward Carpenter asks: " Who is there so unfortunate as not to have had the experience, in ordinary daily life, of seeing some features, perhaps those of a well-known person, suddenly transformed, with the strangest possible sense of transcendent Presence? " It is from such moments that the artist, in plastic art, in fiction, and in music is giving us new arrangements of old familiars, old familiars in new guises as different, surely, as the allotrope of water, whatever that allotrope proves to be, will be from water itself.

Those whose idea of art is a raft to rescue them from reality have not welcomed these revaluations. All that they now face in novels they have been accustomed to sense uncomfortably in newspapers and in life, but when they picked up " a good book," they wanted help in forgetting themselves. They had mistaken the sense of security for art. This is perfect as rest, but bad as a foundation of literary taste. Yet this type of reader has made this criticism again and again down the years, because the type has always been slow to recognize any extension of freedom.

It is an extension of freedom upon which the novel has entered, nothing more alarming; that which in art, as in the movement of peoples, and of the general mind and spirit of the race, has always been the goal. All that is happening to the novel, to poetry, to plastic art, to music, has happened over and over again to art, as to politics, to religion, to human relationship. But the search for freedom has a technique. When the technique is not regarded, freedom is formless or it altogether fails. And the chief article of this technique is not inclusion. It is selection. We did not advance from *Clarissa Harlowe* to *Ethan Frome* by including in novels everything which might be included. The commonplace, the evil, the ugly are not necessarily suitable material for a novel, no matter how free the novel form finds itself. The novel has of course advanced partly by omissions — " re-

fining by so much as he chiseled away," Pater
says of his craftsman. The novel advances by
extending its sources of material. But it arrives
by selection.

The process of writing a novel involves: (1)
The quickening within of something to be expressed. (2) The nourishing of that impulse.
(3) The development of a technique of expression. All three processes involve both freedom
and a selective use of that freedom.

Here we have a tentative outline of the process of any art expression: the quickening, the
feeding, the technique. But this also is the process of education — the quickening, the feeding,
the technique. And this is not less the story of
the ideal of government — the quickening
of the social impulse, the feeding of the social
impulse, the technique of the expression of the
social impulse. And religion, regarding it —
as Mr. A. R. Orage has called it — as the process of the divinization of man, proceeds in the
same fashion: the quickening, the feeding, the
technique. Art is not more a process of creation than the processes of education, of government, of divinization. All must proceed both
by freedom and a selective use of that freedom. Thus scholarship, government, religion,
and art are all in the domain of the creative
— all should be primarily powers of expression, of life more abundant.

II

Passing by government and divinization as improper subjects for social intercourse, consider the slow encroachments of everyday branches of the curricula upon realms of the creative. We have long been accustomed to this process in physics — in physics, which used to be considered pure scholarship, and in the Middle Ages was classed as an occult science, and then became the servant of man. Now we have yesterday's discovery of the new substance called fused quartz, which can send light and heat round a curve. There, in the laboratories of the General Electric in Lynn, Massachusetts, they hold a rod of the fused quartz, heat one end of it, and while the rod itself remains cold, the other end will shower the heat. And it is said to permit the passage of the ultra-violet rays, so that through its lamps we shall be independent of the sunlight and grow green plants which never see the sun. This is another step in that list of adventures which we may fairly call creative physics. In botany, surely all that advance which we loosely class as Burbankism is as creative as song. In geometry we have abandoned sobriety altogether and have entered joyfully upon fantasy under that stretched word " relativity "; and when expression fails us, we have always the two words " fourth dimensional " —

these mean something too, even as Horace prophesied of words, that new meanings should creep in and possess them. And if there is a creative course in the universities, it is now psychology, though barely ten years ago the psychologists were saying that the human mind was charted, that *there*, at any rate, we should know nothing more.

It is true that all these adventures are but the uncovering of inner conditions and relationships — but that is what art is. Art does not invent. It reveals.

Here, for example, is architectural ornament as creative as Burbankism itself! For a most thrilling study of what is afoot in this domain, I commend to you a vast slim book lately issued by the American Institute of Architects — Louis Sullivan's *A System of Architectural Ornament — According with a Philosophy of Man's Powers* . . . with a prelude and interlude which are not less than poetry; its theory that the seat of power is the will to life in every creative worker; and its plates of geometrical figures so beautiful that you see them with the pang of a look at the ephemeral — and yet they are as eternal as the sky and as bourgeoning as the spring. And one will have such a caption as this: " Development of a blank block illustrating man's control over materials and their destiny " — a block growing from a dead cube to the quickened beauty of line and curve and star and trefoil — a child's block, evolving to an ornament of exquisite beauty. Then simple leaf-forms, the elm, the apple, the clover, rising to unimagined loveliness of form by springing line and whorl and tendril woven in gracious patterns about the central motif, " following," he says, " following nature's method of liberating energy." You can never again look at a leaf without seeing nature dreaming in maple and chestnut toward what Edgar Saltus called " excesses of grace." Perhaps the Sullivans dreaming new leaves and new adventures in line shall find their Burbanks to develop the potential and eternal energy of form. Then a page of pentagons, simple, expressionless, sleeping, then darting lines cutting their edges, crossing their surfaces, winging out from their angles, until there comes a page plate of something breathlessly lovely, something like crystals and ferns and lightning and the curve of rainbows and the rhythm of echoes — a beautiful entity. And the rigid original figure has vanished " in a mobile medium." He calls it plastic geometry, he calls it the Awakening of the Pentagon. We might call it — an allotrope of the pentagon. Plate after plate of beauty, and you wonder why our rugs and our wall-paper and our lamp-shades and children's play-rooms cannot be offered to us in these lovely guises. . . .

One caption says: " There being no limit to the field of character expression, this design lies within the field of romance." You look and you know that halos of saints and crowns of kings represent actual structural beauty of line emanating from purity or from power in life, in human energy. You look — and you know that the outline of the Holy Grail itself grew out of some such conception of structural beauty momentarily uncovered to an eye of sufficient purity and power to perceive it. You understand the symbolism of the Host. You look — and you see in these figures approximations of the human form — and you realize with a thrill that our very bodies come under these laws of possible beauty and graciousness. That our bodies are walking the earth like figures of clay when they might be radiating loveliness, flashing atmospheres of beauty and graciousness — allotropes of the flesh. Yet once architecture was merely the raising of a shelter from the elements, the dry routine of draughtsmen earning a livelihood — no more of a creative art than that.

And then for all our adventures, see what remains untouched. The whole phenomenon of sound — what do we know of it? Acoustics is a mystery to modify which we use incantations of a stretched wire. Certain sounds produce madness in animals. From Alexander

down, music has the potency of witchcraft
— yet what do we guess of the power of
sound? If the walls of Jericho did fall down to
trumpets, we shall not know it yet. For all the
revelations concerning the subconscious, who
shall be explicit about the reason that we
can will to wake at a certain hour, and
wake at that hour. Suggestion to the subconscious, yes — but *what happens?* Our
explanations are as generic as that of the Yel-
lowstone Park guide, seeking to account for
the geysers. Said he: " I think this whole region was either let down or hove up." Yet
thirty years ago Charles Godfrey Leland was
saying that our drudgery of learning was already an anachronism, and that in time the
whole routine of education, as we know it
now, would be superseded by the autosugges-
tive process; by *la Volonté.* For that matter
what, explicitly, is the process of rebuilding
which goes forward during sleep? We sleep
for five minutes and say that we wake in-
credibly refreshed; but what, categorically,
has happened? And who shall say that the
significance of this slow intaking and outgo-
ing of the breath of the body and of the spirit
is even remotely divined? Nothing in creation
as we know it now is more mysterious than
that rhythmic foundation of moment-to-mo-
ment life. Nothing unless it is our dying. But
dying occasionally is given all the importance

of art itself, as when in Paris there arose a society, of which Madame Curie was one of the
sponsors, organized " for the study of the
phenomenon of death." . . . Unabashed by
the mysteries of death and breath and sleep,
we believe that we know all about our bodies.
We will hardly listen when they tell us that
they are permeated by a new substance, in-
terpenetrating the physical body; and when
they make known that this substance reveals
different colors; and when it is suggested that
behavior and mental attitude may condition
those colors. When we deride such a new form
of substance, we are asked in an article in
Harper's Magazine to remember how lately it
was that Benjamin Franklin appeared before
the British Royal Society and announced to
the members that there existed a new form of
energy; and they solemnly ridiculed him. (We
can forgive them, though. Not one of the
members of the British Royal Society of that
day could have read *Ethan Frome* or *Joanna
Godden* or *Antoinette Toner* or any of Joseph
Conrad.)

By our derisions and our incredulities of
these things, we are irresistibly reminded of
that Kentucky school-board which once de-
nied the use of its building for a discussion of
the new invention of the locomotive engine;
" for," said the document, " if God had in-
tended man to go at any such speed as fifteen

miles an hour, there would have been something about it in the Bible."

And of Daniel Webster's Congressional speech opposing the building of the first transcontinental railroad. And when he had pictured the terrors of the Great American Desert, the impassivity of the Rocky Mountains, the impracticability of settling that barren coast, with its useless harbors, he concluded: " No, gentlemen! Not one dollar of United States money shall ever be spent, with my consent, to bring the Pacific Coast one mile nearer to Boston."

It is as if creative energy were constantly furthering a new rate of vibration in life, reflecting in some new and even outlandish response of man to his surroundings, the same old familiar miraculous surroundings and relationships, about which he is forever discerning more. Sometimes these awakenings have come softly, in Italy, in Greece, in England, in Palestine, in Thibet — shy dawns on the hills or flaming suns across the miles. And now, in the confusion of the world, we are nevertheless in a period of intense response to this eternal outpouring of creative energy. When Professor George Santayana says that civilization may be approaching one of those long winters which overtake us from time to time; that a flood of barbarism may soon overwhelm all the work of our ancestors, as another flood two thousand years ago overwhelmed that of the ancients, it may be that his new flood is as mythical as the old one. For even so must geometrical figures in general react when they see an immobile pentagon awakening to plastic life. And picture the emotions of fused quartz when it feels heat and light passing through its own cold length and escaping in glory! Even consider us, divining afar off, and occasionally, glimpses of allotropes of ourselves.

The allotropes of ourselves. Why not? What if man's persistent belief in his own spirit is his divination of his own allotrope, waiting in his flesh to be at last released from that ambiguous laboratory? What if every one of his faculties, with which he muddles along, has in reality this other potential functioning, according to some deeper law, by which it could contact and express as much more beauty as an awakened pentagon can express over a blind block. Already the creators in plastic and pictorial art have seen a stranger and a lovelier world than you and I see — a world which is actually here — only we have coal sight and cannot see it, cannot vision that light and line and distance.

To a fourteenth-century monk, bending over his manuscript, and copying it by hand, came Mercury, who said: " It shall soon go, that manuscript, under the sea and through the air, to a land of which you have never even heard, and there, by a process which you do not know, it shall be multiplied by the million and shot forth over miles of fine wire and lengths of steel, and be read by thousands of eyes, it may be at one time." And without even raising his eyes to Mercury, the monk said: "What you say is impossible. Do you not see that I have here the only copy of this manuscript in existence? You speak of an illusion."

When allotropes of tomorrow try to get themselves discovered, in perception or in opinion, allotropes which seem to deny the scholarship of today, or to transcend its art, we need not believe — belief is too much to ask. But we are not forced to be fourteenth-century monks.

Not all of us is incarnate. Some of us is spirit. And it is required of us that we see ourselves both in flesh and in spirit all the time.

CHAPTER XII

Two Summaries

I. BEYOND BEHAVIORISM
II. THE THREE CONVENTIONS

BEYOND BEHAVIORISM

ONE WHO IS CONTENT with automatism as the answer to the riddle of ourselves will be interested in *Beyond Behaviorism* by Robert Courtney. But one who grants the whole mechanistic implication and who yet concedes that possibly we may not know all, will find here a place to rest his foot above the waters. He may even return with an indication of more dry land. And further he will find hints toward a technique for abandoning the biological and sociological ark which he has naïvely believed to constitute his universe.

The anxious attempt to delay the threatened collapse of civilization by producing bigger and better men through education and through eugenics is a faint hope for the sports of environment and heredity. Wurzberg and functionalism, Titchener and structuralism, the Gestalt movement, Watson and behaviorism, the final placing of psychology upon the plane of the other sciences, and the description of behavior in scientific chemico-physical terms leave little room for the " will " and the " soul " of man. And since connected sequences of muscle tensions make up his content and determine whether he shall be

practical, æsthetic, or intellectual; and since
he is a biological product of the three inter-
acting systems, muscular, visceral, and cerebral; and since he is a biped with a
" conditioned response " and no more, this
biped's age-old dream that he has a soul becomes a wish-fulfillment, and is ministered to
by an eager " democratic decadence of original
ethics into altruism." For by a figurative en-
largement of the visceral system no man can
become a god. The bigger and better man,
the superman as we used to say, will be no different in kind, but different merely in degree. The saint, the ascetic, the yogi are all,
equally with the rest of mankind, automata.

But now Mr. Courtney says that which the
pioneers of all ages say, that there must be
some escape. From this *cul-de-sac* of mechan-
ically habitized action man must free himself
as he has earlier freed himself from a fireless,
toolless, and wordless world. There are always
those whom neither day-dreams nor extinc-
tion can satisfy. Mr. Courtney calls the attention of these, " casting about for a hint however slender," to that which, seventy-five pages
back, he has made the subject of his opening
chapter: Psyche, the butterfly. The butterfly,
a larva, an invertebrate; then a blob of creamy
liquid, the chrysalis; then an aerial life — " *in
which remains no remnant of the worm.*"

Not in growth, but in metamorphic development he hazards our course to lie. No exaggerations of the characteristics of the worm, but " some fourth possibility, in addition to the three now exercised by man, the muscular, the visceral, and the cerebral," which " present that unbroken front of mechanistic operation." Nature brings about the butterfly's transformation, but nature does no such service for us. This we must do for ourselves.

But what do we mean by " ourselves." Do we mean that all-inclusive instrument, our body? Our verbalization that *we* have decided something means — it has been shown by the mechanists — that it is some subordinate physical structure of our organism which has come to a foreordained decision. " We say ' I this ' and ' I that,' *thereby employing a convention devoid of meaning, since it implicitly denies an inclusive automatism which is actual.*"

In short, a means is needed whereby " I " can " begin its existence as an actual entity," whereby the now empty word may conceivably commence to achieve a meaning which is real. A meaning by which " I " may be isolated, with completely impersonal non-identification, from its behaving body. However:

Assuredly, " I " cannot at once, if ever, aspire to the control of this complicated organism behind which stand millions of years of biological and sociological history. But " I " can at least maintain from the outset an occasional brief, independent existence in just the way " I " can observe, in the sense of being vividly aware of, the contemporary actions of the powerful machine, the body, to which " I " find myself accountably attached. This " I " can begin its own existence by beginning independently to gather its own understanding of the mechanism it, perhaps, hopes eventually to control for the purpose of effecting through it, not sociological automatized, but free individualized action.

Starting with a quotation from an old manuscript, " The Only Way," Mr. Courtney indicates the technique of a new function whose basis of " attention," of " awareness," he outlines as sanely as he has accepted behaviorism for the three known sets of functions of man. For this unexercised faculty, by means of which direct knowledge of our own body is obtainable, he notes the term " apprehension " as proposed by Professor Whitehead in *Science and the Modern World*, and distinguished from " apprehension " of external objects, including our own bodies in their spatial and functional relationships.

" Do we," Mr. Courtney asks, " normally exercise this activity? We do not; it has never even occurred to us. But can we do so? Most certainly we can."

Just as sensations are received into the physical-muscular system and form its content, so, he suggests, these impressions may begin to fill another physical system with content, thereby actualizing it; that is, enabling it to function. Only three systems have been found in the human organism by science. But are these all? For how recently has science divined the glands of internal secretion, and ceased assuring us that one of them was the vestigial remains of an eye.

The elaboration of this dawning functioning, this gesture toward the nature of a developed " I," able to isolate its bodily functions from itself and to begin to define itself, together with certain probable results of the process, these occupy the remainder of the book. This possible key " whose existence mankind has always profoundly suspected " (and in consequence of which has been so lenient with counterfeits), this hypothesis that potentialities of consciousness may be actualized, may have been " the basis of much ancient and religious lore, from early Buddhism to alchemy." And this inauguration of a fourth activity on the part of human beings — namely, a current " awareness " of the muscular, visceral, and cerebral activities — this listening, by the conductor of the orchestra, to all his instruments, this wresting from nature " our " rightful authority, long usurped by heredity and environment, biology and sociology, is concerned with a perception different *in kind* from any sort of perception ordinarily used by human beings.

The expansion takes place within, in a direction toward which we should never have thought to look, and compared to it our trivial attempts to perceive more and more of the three old dimensions are meager indeed. " When we think of the efforts put forth to achieve external expansion by aeroplane, cinema, and radio, we realize how great is the desire of mankind for increased consciousness." But by far the greatest increase must come, not by a quantitative addition to what is already possessed in three dimensions, but by the conquering of an entirely new direction of consciousness — " the direction of within-ness."

The sharpest insistence is made upon the distinction between " awareness " and introspection. The introspective method, as put forward by James and his followers, is determined by the cerebral operation of the very machine it seeks to know; for " the normal use of the cerebral system, like the muscular and emotional, is toward the outside world, and its reversal ends in distortion. On the other hand, the faculty not of thought but of awareness can only be used within; that is *its* normal use."

This hypothesis which, in his foreword, Mr.

Courtney credits to another,[1] can at any rate be pragmatically tested by everybody. If it works, it may be the meeting-ground of science and religion; for it would be the passing from the last of our mechanistic functions now known to the first of the conscious functioning of our old friend and complete stranger, " I."

THE THREE CONVENTIONS

THAT THERE IS NOW awaiting man a world of Reality to be experienced when he shall have rendered himself fine enough to receive it is the word of Professor Denis Saurat's *The Three Conventions*, and he ventures to point not a program, but a path.

Mr. A. R. Orage in the book's compact and revealing preface, suggests that if, according to the general assumption of modern science, that which we call life is only Becoming, then metaphysics and philosophy proper may well be regarded as unworthy of serious attention; but if, on the other hand, life is not the process of the Becoming of Reality, but only of our Perception of Reality, much that is now necessarily unintelligible becomes at least potentially intelligible. A superior perception of to-day could in fact divine something of the ground-floor pattern. The truth would be comparable to mathematics and the noumena of Being would be visible behind the phenomena of Becoming.

This classical assumption of life as man's progressive perception of Reality is the assumption of Professor Saurat; and for the quickening of that perception he proposes that man shall emerge from the lax comfort — or the elementary struggles — of idealism into directed action. Beside his exact and considered pronouncements, idealism as men proudly espouse it becomes a slipshod and spineless preoccupation. Rather, it is seen as the effort of the self to give some intimation which it has independently received of the tremendous adventure upon which mankind is engaged; but in receiving such intimations mankind has interpreted them by two ancient "conventions," and must now proceed to the creation of the third "convention."

The two ancient conventions are the Material and the Moral. The Material or universal convention discovered physical laws. The Moral convention discovered moral laws. The next task is the discovery of the convention of ideas, a Metaphysical convention. For though we now have a body of physical laws that are true for all things, and as there is "more or less" a body of moral laws true for all men, so there must be a body of ideas true for all minds. "But as yet there are only individual minds," with no established and conscious relationship to a body of ideas on which they can depend, as they now depend on the laws of gravitation and hydraulics, of honesty and justice.

The very thing therefore on which we pride ourselves, is thus regarded by Professor Saurat as a limitation. " As yet there are *only* individual minds." Our precious power to go off at a tangent is questioned. As no man any longer claims for himself the ability to say that there is no such thing as gravitation, or that electricity is a matter of opinion; and as no man would contend that the wages of sin is life more abundant continuously; just so a sovereign power to say that this or that idea is not a truth, the most liberty-loving individual is to relinquish. For in ideas, the author implies, we are still exactly where the Philistine is in art: " I don't know what is true, but I know what is true for me and I continue to like it and shall follow it and moreover shall expect to be called a fine fellow for my courage."

It is this whole Philistine attitude toward ideas from which Professor Saurat sharply diverges, and the slender book is a series of dialogues among psychologist, poet, dreamer, metaphysician, to clarify the need of the search for this third, or Metaphysical, convention.

His intimation as to how this search is to be begun is slight, but it is clear. The raw material for the creation of this World of Ideas is desires. Again the process is seen to be scientific. Just as chemical elements cannot be utilized until they are broken down, so raw desires are but crudely utilizable until they are subdivided and resolved into ideas. For example, the progress of the sex desire in the race, as in the individual, registers its transformation into many needs, many ideas " of beauty, intensity, expansion, of high action," the original desire coming back " in new modes of being and expression, in ideas with their infinitely more rapid rhythm."

Beside the useful bunglings of Freud naïvely affirming the opposite, that such ideas and needs are but the makeshift expressions of desire, these adult utterances of Professor Saurat seem affirmations for a world which has come of age, and knows ideas as its proper food. Other desires also must be broken down into ideas and then organized. How? There is only this intimation: that which is expressed Professor Saurat calls the Actual. That which remains unexpressed he called the Inactual. Man has now to concentrate on the Inactual, perhaps even to make a further manifestation of a further God, even as already he has acknowledged a God as Creator of the world, " and of the material convention," and Messiahs as founders of the Moral convention.

All this leads into countless enchanting areas. As to that of immortality, which becomes no more than a by-product of the third convention; and skepticism as to immortality seems merely the *gauche* admission of the egoist intent on his immediate visible personal self, having but the two old conventions. And this applies to the immortality of worlds.

The delicacy of the book suggests the newest handlings of light, illumination as integration rather than as accessory. The fineness is in the fiber of the fabric of both content and style. In a determined pressing back of old barriers, there is no gesture, no bravado, not that unsatisfied passion for delicacy which masks as indelicacy, never the Puritanism which seeks equilibrium by denying its own motion. His delicacy never receives his own attention, but of it he seems unaware.

The book is of the utmost importance. In its restatement of a classic divination, it becomes the last word in the science of discovering the nature of being. In its modernity, if it could reach the chaos of the young intellectual, he would be the first to take to himself its cool and detached discoveries. Growing bored by his own desires, it is possible that he might be lured to this world of ideas — not for a research, but for a satisfaction.

A NOTE ON THE TYPE IN
WHICH THIS BOOK IS SET

This book is set on the Linotype in Garamont, a modern rendering of the type first cut in the sixteenth century by Claude Garamond (1510–1561). He was a pupil of Geofroy Tory and is believed to have based his letters on the Venetian models although he introduced a number of important differences, and it is to him we owe the letter which we know as Old Style. He gave to his letters a certain elegance and a feeling of movement which won for their creator an immediate reputation and the patronage of the French King, Francis I.

SET UP, ELECTROTYPED, PRINTED AND BOUND BY THE PLIMPTON PRESS, NORWOOD, MASS. PAPER MANUFACTURED BY CURTIS AND BROTHER, NEWARK, DELAWARE. · THE FRONTISPIECE IS A WOODCUT BY RICHARD BENNETT. · THE AMBROTYPE OF ELIZA BEERS AT PAGE 71 WAS PRINTED IN AQUATONE BY EDWARD STERN & COMPANY, PHILADELPHIA. · THE BINDING WAS DESIGNED BY W. A. DWIGGINS